CLASSIC
RECIPES™

Publications International, Ltd.
Favorite Brand Name Recipes at www.fbnr.com

Microwave Cooking: Microwave ovens vary in wattage. Use the cooking times as guidelines and check for doneness before adding more time.

Preparation/Cooking Times: Preparation times are based on the approximate amount of time required to assemble the recipe before cooking, baking, chilling or serving. These times include preparation steps such as measuring, chopping and mixing. The fact that some preparations and cooking can be done simultaneously is taken into account. Preparation of optional ingredients and serving suggestions is not included.

Table of Contents

All the recipes appearing in this publication have been developed and carefully tested by the food professionals in the BAKER'S Test Kitchens. We created the recipes so you'll get rave reviews when you prepare them for your friends and family. Included also are BAKER'S tips to help you get perfect results every time.

TIPS AND TECHNIQUES

Storing Chocolate

Store chocolate in a cool, dry place, below 75°F, if possible. At higher temperatures, the cocoa butter melts and rises to the surface. When this happens, the chocolate develops a pale, gray color called "bloom." This condition does not affect the flavor or quality of the chocolate in any way. The original color will return when the chocolate is melted.

Chocolate Substitutions

Most recipes are carefully developed and tested so that you can be assured of successful results only if you follow the recipe exactly. Do not substitute sweet or semi-sweet chocolate for unsweetened and vice versa. Bittersweet chocolate can be substituted for semi-sweet chocolate. For semi-sweet and white chocolate chunks:

1 cup (6 ounces) chocolate chunks = 6 squares, chopped
1 bag (12 ounces) chocolate chunks =12 squares, chopped

Melting Chocolate

The BAKER'S Test Kitchens highly recommend using the microwave method for melting chocolate whenever possible. Chocolate scorches easily on top of the stove; use very low heat and a heavy saucepan.

To melt chocolate squares in the microwave oven, place unwrapped chocolate in a microwavable bowl. For 1 square of chocolate, microwave on HIGH 1 to 2 minutes or until almost melted, stirring after each minute. Remove from the microwave. Stir until completely melted. Add 10 seconds for each additional square of chocolate.

When melting chocolate alone, use a completely dry container and stirring utensil. Even a tiny drop of moisture can cause the chocolate to tighten (become coarse-textured and clump together). If this happens, add 1 teaspoon solid shortening (not butter or margarine) for each square of chocolate. Stir until smooth. Some recipes call for melting chocolate with liquids. It is a matter of proportions: a lot of liquid will not tighten the chocolate, but a little will.

EASY CHOCOLATE GARNISHES

Try these finishing touches to make your recipes extra-special.

Grating Chocolate

Grate 1 square BAKER'S Semi-Sweet or White Chocolate or $1/2$ package BAKER'S GERMAN'S Sweet Chocolate over the large holes of a hand grater.

Shaving Chocolate

Warm 1 wrapped square of BAKER'S Semi-Sweet or White Chocolate or a 3-square strip of BAKER'S GERMAN'S Sweet Chocolate by holding it in the palm of your hand. Pull a vegetable peeler across the surface of the square. Sprinkle grated or shaved chocolate over cakes, pies or desserts.

Chocolate Curls

Melt 4 squares BAKER'S Semi-Sweet or White Chocolate or 1 package (4 ounces) BAKER'S GERMAN'S Sweet Chocolate. Spread with a spatula into a very thin layer on a cookie sheet. Refrigerate until firm but still pliable, about 10 minutes.

To make curls, slip the tip of a straight-side metal spatula under the chocolate. Push the spatula firmly along the cookie sheet, under the chocolate, so the chocolate curls as it is pushed. (If chocolate is too firm to curl, let stand a few minutes at room temperature; refrigerate again if it becomes too soft.) Carefully pick up each chocolate curl by inserting a wooden pick in the center. Lift onto a waxed paper-lined cookie sheet. Refrigerate until firm, about 15 minutes. Use a wooden pick to arrange curls on dessert.

Grated and shaved chocolate and chocolate curls may be stored in the freezer in an airtight container for up to 6 months.

Chocolate Drizzle

Place 1 square BAKER'S Semi-Sweet or White Chocolate in a small zipper-style plastic bag. Close the bag tightly. Microwave on HIGH about 1 minute until chocolate is melted. Fold down the top of the bag tightly and snip a tiny piece off 1 corner (about $1/8$ inch).

Holding the top of the bag tightly, drizzle chocolate through the opening over the dessert.

Chocolate Doodles

Melt chocolate following directions for Chocolate Drizzle. Drizzle chocolate into free-form designs onto waxed paper-lined cookie sheet. (Or draw design on paper cover with waxed paper and drizzle chocolate over design.) Refrigerate until firm, about 30 minutes. Use as garnish for cakes and other desserts.

Chocolate Cups

Melt 1 package (8 ounces) BAKER'S Semi-Sweet Chocolate. Spread chocolate over the inside of 10 aluminum foil baking cups or double-layered paper baking cups using a spoon or brush to completely coat all surfaces with a layer of chocolate. Set cups in muffin pans. Refrigerate until firm, about 1 hour. (Small bon bon cups may also be used.) Holding cup in one hand, carefully peel off paper or aluminum foil. Refrigerate until ready to use.

Chocolate Leaves

Melt 4 squares BAKER'S Semi-Sweet Chocolate or 1 package (4 ounces) BAKER'S GERMAN'S Sweet Chocolate. Using a narrow spatula or brush, spread chocolate over undersides of washed and dried non-toxic leaves (such as lemon, rose or grape ivy) to form smooth, thick coating. Avoid spreading chocolate to very edge of leaf to prevent chocolate from running onto top side of leaf. Place leaves on waxed paper-lined tray. Refrigerate until chocolate is firm, about 15 minutes. Carefully peel away leaves from chocolate. Refrigerate chocolate leaves until ready to use.

Chocolate Cutouts

Melt 4 squares BAKER'S Semi-Sweet Chocolate or 1 package (4 ounces) BAKER'S GERMAN'S Sweet Chocolate. Pour onto waxed paper-lined cookie sheet; spread to $1/8$-inch thickness with spatula. Refrigerate until firm, about 15 minutes. Cut out shapes with cookie cutters. Immediately lift shapes carefully from waxed paper with spatula or knife. Refrigerate until ready to use.

BAKER'S CHOCOLATE PRODUCTS

GERMAN'S Sweet Chocolate was created by Samuel German in 1852 as a quality snack-type chocolate. It's a special blend of chocolate, enriched with cocoa butter and sugar.

White Chocolate is made with cocoa butter, milk and sugar, without the cocoa solids, making it creamy white in color and mild and sweet in flavor.

Bittersweet Chocolate is a mixture of chocolate liquor, additional cocoa butter and sugar. It is blended to have a more pronounced European-style chocolate flavor and a higher chocolate liquor content.

BAKER'S Chocolate Chunks in Semi-Sweet, Milk and White varieties can be used in many of the recipes included in the book. These premium chocolate chunks are made especially for indulgent cookies, brownies and other desserts.

Unsweetened Chocolate is made from a blend of fine cocoa beans—roasted, crushed and ground between large heated rollers to form this purest form of chocolate—satin-smooth and rich in cocoa butter. Nothing is added or removed from this fragrant chocolate mixture, called chocolate liquor.

Semi-Sweet Chocolate is made from the same rich chocolate liquor, with just enough sugar, cocoa butter and vanilla added to give a rich, sweet taste.

BAKER'S CHOCOLATE HISTORY

BAKER'S Chocolate enjoys a sweet history that started before the American Revolution! In 1765, a Massachusetts physician, Dr. James Baker, went into partnership with a young Irish chocolate-maker, John Hannon. Together, they started America's first chocolate mill, where, in 1780, they made a blend of quality chocolate called BAKER'S chocolate. When John Hannon died, Dr. Baker took over the mill and it became a family enterprise. In 1824, James' grandson Walter became head of the business.

The high standards of the Baker family have continued to the present. That's why over the years, Americans have learned to rely on the continuing quality of BAKER'S Chocolate. They look for the BAKER'S label with its charming signature lady. And that leads us to another story....

Gracing each package of BAKER'S Chocolate products since the 18th Century is the lovely silhouette of La Belle Chocolatiere—the beautiful chocolate waitress. How La Belle came to be on BAKER'S packages is a fairy tale...Once upon a time, a prince visited a Viennese chocolate house where a beautiful young waitress served him. As the tale goes, he fell in love with her and married her. The prince had her portrait painted and it later hung in the Dresden Museum. The president of BAKER'S Chocolate following the death of Walter Baker was Henry Pierce. He saw the portrait and was determined that it become a symbol of the company. In 1882, this came to pass and La Belle Chocolatiere has been the trademark on all BAKER'S Chocolate ever since.

Decadent Cakes

From luscious layer cakes to creamy cheesecakes, there's something for every chocolate lover in this chapter.

Molten Mocha Cakes

1 package BAKER'S® Semi-Sweet Baking Chocolate
1 cup (2 sticks) butter
2 cups powdered sugar
$^1/_2$ cup GENERAL FOODS INTERNATIONAL COFFEES®,
    any flavor
5 eggs
4 egg yolks
$^3/_4$ cup flour
    Powdered sugar (optional)
    Raspberries (optional)

HEAT oven to 425°F. Butter eight $^3/_4$-cup custard cups or soufflé dishes. Place on cookie sheet.

MICROWAVE chocolate and butter in large microwavable bowl on HIGH 2 minutes or until butter is melted. Stir with wire whisk until chocolate is completely melted. Stir in sugar and flavored instant coffee until well blended. Whisk in eggs and egg yolks. Stir in flour. Divide batter among custard cups.

BAKE 14 to 15 minutes or until sides are firm but centers are soft. Let stand 1 minute, then run small knife around cakes to loosen. Invert cakes onto dessert dishes. Sprinkle with powdered sugar and garnish with raspberries, if desired. *Makes 8 cakes*

Make-Ahead: Bake as directed above. Cool slightly, then cover custard cups with plastic wrap. Refrigerate up to 2 days. Place custard cups on cookie sheet. Reheat in 425°F oven for 12 to 13 minutes.

Prep Time: 15 minutes
Bake Time: 15 minutes

Intensely Chocolate Mousse Cake

$^3/_4$ cup water

$^1/_2$ cup sugar

$^1/_2$ cup corn syrup

$^1/_4$ cup cornstarch

1 $^1/_2$ packages (9 squares) BAKER'S® Bittersweet Baking Chocolate,
coarsely chopped

$^1/_4$ teaspoon salt

$^1/_4$ cup ($^1/_2$ stick) butter *or* margarine

3 large eggs, at room temperature, lightly beaten

1 cup whipping (heavy) cream

Boiling water

GREASE and flour 9-inch springform pan. Stir water, sugar, corn syrup and cornstarch in heavy 4- or 6-quart saucepan. Cook on low heat, stirring constantly, until sugar is dissolved. Add chocolate and salt; increase heat to medium. Continue cooking, stirring constantly, until chocolate is melted and just about to come to boil. Remove from heat.

STIR in butter until melted. Transfer mixture to large bowl. Refrigerate 15 minutes, stirring occasionally, until mixture has cooled (may still be warm to the touch). Heat oven to 350°F.

WHISK eggs into chocolate mixture. Beat cream with electric mixer on medium speed until soft peaks form. Gently fold whipped cream into chocolate mixture. Spoon mixture into prepared pan. Place pan in larger baking pan, then place on center rack in oven. Carefully pour boiling water to come halfway up side of springform pan.

BAKE 45 minutes or until mixture is just set. Top will feel slightly firm to the touch. Run small knife or spatula around rim of pan to loosen cake; cool before removing rim of pan. Cover top with plastic wrap and refrigerate 4 hours or overnight. *Makes 12 servings*

Prep Time: 20 minutes
Bake Time: 45 minutes
Refrigerate Time: 4 hours

To serve, use a large sharp knife to cut cake into
slices, wiping blade of knife between cuts.

White Chocolate Raspberry Cake

1 package (6 squares) BAKER'S® Premium White Baking
   Chocolate, chopped

$^1/_2$ cup (1 stick) butter *or* margarine

1 package (2-layer size) white cake mix

1 cup milk

3 eggs

1 teaspoon vanilla

White Chocolate Cream Cheese Frosting (recipe page 16)

2 tablespoons seedless raspberry jam

1 cup raspberries

HEAT oven to 350°F. Grease and flour 2 (9-inch) round cake pans; set aside.

MICROWAVE chocolate and butter in medium microwavable bowl on HIGH 2 minutes or until butter is melted. Stir until chocolate is completely melted; cool slightly.

BEAT cake mix, milk, eggs, vanilla and chocolate mixture in large bowl with electric mixer on low speed just until moistened, scraping side of bowl often. Beat on medium speed 2 minutes or until well blended. Pour into prepared pans.

BAKE 25 to 28 minutes or until toothpick inserted in centers comes out clean. Cool cakes in pans 10 minutes; remove from pans. Cool completely on wire rack.

PLACE 1 cake layer on serving plate. Spread with $^2/_3$ cup of the frosting, then jam. Place second cake layer on top. Frost top and side with remaining frosting. Garnish with raspberries.   *Makes 12 to 16 servings*

continued on page 16

White Chocolate Raspberry Cake

White Chocolate Raspberry Cake, continued

Marbled White Chocolate Raspberry Cake: Prepare batter as directed. Remove 1 cup batter to small bowl. Stir in 2 tablespoons seedless raspberry jam and 2 drops red food coloring. Spoon remaining batter into prepared pans. Place spoonfuls of pink batter into each pan. Swirl with small knife to marbleize. Bake as directed.

Prep Time: 30 minutes
Bake Time: 28 minutes

White Chocolate Cream Cheese Frosting

- 1 package (8 ounces) PHILADELPHIA® Cream Cheese, softened
- 4 tablespoons (¹/₂ stick) butter *or* margarine, softened
- 1 package (6 ounces) BAKER'S® Premium White Baking Chocolate, melted, cooled slightly
- 1 teaspoon vanilla
- 2 cups powdered sugar

BEAT cream cheese and butter in large bowl with electric mixer on medium speed until well blended. Add melted chocolate and vanilla; beat until blended.

BEAT in sugar until light and fluffy.   *Makes 3 cups*

Prep Time: 10 minutes

16

Chocolate Swirl Cheesecake

2 packages (8 ounces each) PHILADELPHIA® Cream Cheese, softened, divided

$^1/_2$ cup sugar, divided

2 eggs, divided

4 squares BAKER'S® Semi-Sweet Baking Chocolate, melted, slightly cooled

1 OREO® Pie Crust (6 ounces or 9 inch)

$^1/_2$ teaspoon vanilla

HEAT oven to 350°F.

BEAT 1 package of the cream cheese, $^1/_4$ cup of the sugar and 1 egg in large bowl with electric mixer on medium speed until well blended. Stir in melted chocolate. Pour into crust. Beat remaining $^1/_4$ cup cream cheese, sugar, egg and vanilla until well blended. Spoon over chocolate batter; swirl with knife to marbleize.

BAKE 40 minutes or until center is almost set. Cool completely on wire rack.

REFRIGERATE 3 hours or overnight.   *Makes 8 servings*

Prep Time: 10 minutes
Bake Time: 40 minutes
Refrigerate Time: 3 hours

Café au Lait Cheesecake

4 packages (8 ounces each) PHILADELPHIA® Cream Cheese,
    softened

1 cup sugar

2 teaspoons grated orange peel

4 eggs

$1/3$ cup strong brewed MAXWELL HOUSE® Coffee

1 package (6 squares) BAKER'S® Premium White Baking
    Chocolate, melted, cooled slightly

1 tablespoon cocoa powder

$1/4$ teaspoon cinnamon

HEAT oven to 325°F. Grease 9-inch springform pan.

BEAT cream cheese, sugar and orange peel in large bowl with electric mixer on medium speed until well blended. Add eggs, 1 at a time, beating on low speed after each addition, just until blended. Beat in coffee, then melted chocolate. Pour into prepared pan.

BAKE 55 to 60 minutes or until center is almost set. Run small knife or spatula around rim of pan to loosen cake; cool before removing rim of pan.

REFRIGERATE 4 hours or overnight. Mix cocoa powder and cinnamon; sprinkle over cheesecake. Garnish with chocolate-covered coffee beans, if desired.   *Makes 12 to 16 servings*

To soften cream cheese in the microwave: Place 1 completely unwrapped 8-ounce package of cream cheese in a microwavable bowl. Microwave on HIGH for 15 seconds. Add 15 seconds for each additional package of cream cheese.

Brownie Torte

1 package (6 squares) BAKER'S® Bittersweet Baking Chocolate, divided

³/₄ cup (1 ¹/₂ sticks) butter *or* margarine

1 cup sugar

3 eggs

1 teaspoon vanilla

¹/₃ cup flour

¹/₄ teaspoon salt

¹/₂ cup chopped pecans (optional)

HEAT oven to 350°F. Grease and flour 9-inch round cake pan. Line bottom of pan with wax paper.

MICROWAVE 4 squares of the chocolate and butter in large microwavable bowl on HIGH 2 minutes or until butter is melted. Stir until chocolate is completely melted.

STIR sugar into chocolate mixture until well blended. Mix in eggs and vanilla. Stir in flour and salt until well blended. Stir in nuts. Pour into prepared pan.

BAKE 40 minutes or until toothpick inserted in center comes out with fudgy crumbs. DO NOT OVERBAKE. Cool in pan 5 minutes. Run small knife around side of pan to loosen edge. Invert cake onto serving platter. Remove wax paper. Cool completely. Melt remaining 2 squares of chocolate; drizzle over top of cake. *Makes 12 servings*

Great Substitute: Substitute BAKER'S® Semi-Sweet Baking Chocolate for the Bittersweet Chocolate.

Prep Time: 15 minutes
Bake Time: 40 minutes

German's® Sweet Chocolate Cake

   1 package (4 ounces) BAKER'S® GERMAN'S® Sweet Baking
      Chocolate
$^1/_2$ cup water
   2 cups flour
   1 teaspoon baking soda
$^1/_4$ teaspoon salt
   1 cup (2 sticks) butter *or* margarine, softened
   2 cups sugar
   4 egg yolks
   1 teaspoon vanilla
   1 cup buttermilk
   4 egg whites
   Baker's® Coconut-Pecan Filling and Frosting (recipe page 22)

HEAT oven to 350°F. Line bottoms of three 9-inch layer pans with waxed paper.

MICROWAVE chocolate and water in large microwavable bowl on HIGH $1^1/_2$ to 2 minutes or until chocolate is almost melted, stirring halfway through heating time. Stir until chocolate is completely melted.

MIX flour, baking soda and salt; set aside. Beat butter and sugar in large bowl with electric mixer until light and fluffy. Add egg yolks, one at a time, beating well after each addition. Stir in chocolate and vanilla. Add flour mixture alternately with buttermilk, beating after each addition until smooth.

BEAT egg whites in another large bowl with electric mixer on high speed until stiff peaks form. Gently stir into batter. Pour batter into prepared pans.

BAKE for 30 minutes or until cakes spring back when lightly touched in center.

continued on page 22

German's® Sweet Chocolate Cake

German's® Sweet Chocolate Cake, continued

REMOVE from oven; immediately run spatula between cakes and sides of pans. Cool in pans 15 minutes. Remove from pans; peel off waxed paper. Cool on wire racks.

SPREAD Coconut-Pecan Filling and Frosting between layers and over top of cake.   *Makes 12 servings*

Note: This delicate cake will have a flat, slightly sugary top crust that tends to crack. This is normal and the frosting will cover it up.

Prep Time: 30 minutes
Bake Time: 30 minutes

Coconut-Pecan Filling and Frosting

       1 can (12 ounces) evaporated milk
 1$^1/_2$ cups sugar
  $^3/_4$ cup (1$^1/_2$ sticks) butter *or* margarine
       4 egg yolks, lightly beaten
 1$^1/_2$ teaspoons vanilla
       1 package (7 ounces) BAKER'S® ANGEL FLAKE® Coconut
          (2$^2/_3$ cups)
 1$^1/_2$ cups chopped pecans

STIR milk, sugar, butter, egg yolks and vanilla in saucepan. Cook on medium heat 12 minutes or until thickened and golden brown, stirring constantly. Remove from heat.

STIR in coconut and pecans. Cool to room temperature and spreading consistency.   *Makes about 4$^1/_2$ cups*

Midnight Bliss Cake

1 package (2-layer size) chocolate cake mix, any variety

4 eggs

1 container (8 ounces) BREAKSTONE'S® or KNUDSEN Sour Cream

$^1\!/_2$ cup GENERAL FOODS INTERNATIONAL COFFEES®, any flavor

1 package (4-serving size) JELL-O® Chocolate Flavor Instant Pudding & Pie Filling

$^1\!/_2$ cup oil

$^1\!/_2$ cup water

1 package (8 squares) BAKER'S® Semi-Sweet Baking Chocolate, chopped

HEAT oven to 350°F. Lightly grease and flour 12-cup fluted tube pan or 10-inch tube pan.

BEAT all ingredients except chopped chocolate in large bowl with electric mixer on low speed just until moistened, scraping side of bowl often. Beat on medium speed 2 minutes or until well blended. Stir in chopped chocolate. Pour into prepared pan.

BAKE 50 to 60 minutes or until toothpick inserted near center comes out clean. Cool in pan 10 minutes on wire rack. Loosen cake from sides of pan with small knife or spatula. Invert cake onto rack; gently remove pan. Cool completely on wire rack. Sprinkle with powdered sugar, if desired.

Makes 12 to 16 servings

Great Substitute: Substitute 2 tablespoons MAXWELL HOUSE® Instant Coffee for GENERAL FOODS INTERNATIONAL COFFEES®.

Prep Time: 15 minutes
Bake Time: 60 minutes

Wellesley Fudge Cake

4 squares BAKER'S® Unsweetened Baking Chocolate

1 3/4 cups sugar, divided

1/2 cup water

1 2/3 cups flour

1 teaspoon baking soda

1/4 teaspoon salt

1/2 cup (1 stick) butter *or* margarine, softened

3 eggs

3/4 cup milk

1 teaspoon vanilla

Chocolate Fudge Frosting (recipe page 26)

HEAT oven to 350°F. Grease and flour 2 (9-inch) round cake pans.

MICROWAVE chocolate, 1/2 cup of the sugar and water in large microwavable bowl on HIGH 2 minutes or until chocolate is almost melted. Stir until chocolate is completely melted. Cool to lukewarm.

MIX flour, baking soda and salt; set aside. Beat butter and remaining 1 1/4 cups sugar in large bowl with electric mixer on medium speed until light and fluffy. Add eggs, 1 at a time, beating well after each addition. Add flour mixture alternately with milk, beating after each addition until smooth. Stir in chocolate mixture and vanilla. Pour into prepared pans.

BAKE 30 to 35 minutes or until cakes spring back when lightly touched. Cool cakes in pans 10 minutes; remove from pans. Cool completely on wire racks. Fill and frost with Chocolate Fudge Frosting.

Makes 12 to 16 servings

continued on page 26

Wellesley Fudge Cake

Wellesley Fudge Cake, continued

Chocolate Fudge Frosting

    4 squares BAKER'S® Unsweetened Baking Chocolate
    1 package (16 ounces) powdered sugar (about 4 cups)
    $^1/_2$ cup (1 stick) butter *or* margarine, softened
    2 teaspoons vanilla
    $^1/_3$ cup milk

MICROWAVE chocolate in small microwavable bowl on HIGH
2 minutes. Stir until chocolate is melted and smooth. Cool 5 minutes or
to room temperature.

ADD sugar, butter and vanilla. Gradually beat in milk with electric mixer
on low speed until well blended. If frosting becomes too thick, beat in
additional milk by teaspoonfuls until of spreading consistency.

Makes 3 cups

Prep Time: 30 minutes
Bake Time: 35 minutes

Easy Chocolate Cheesecake

2 packages (8 ounces each) PHILADELPHIA® Cream Cheese, softened
$^1/_2$ cup sugar
$^1/_2$ teaspoon vanilla
2 eggs
4 squares BAKER'S® Semi-Sweet Baking Chocolate, melted, cooled slightly
1 OREO® Pie Crust (9 inch)

HEAT oven to 350°F.

BEAT cream cheese, sugar and vanilla in large bowl with electric mixer on medium speed until well blended. Beat in eggs until blended. Stir in melted chocolate. Pour into crust.

BAKE 40 minutes or until center is almost set. Cool completely on wire rack. Refrigerate 3 hours or overnight. *Makes 8 servings*

Melting Chocolate on Top of Stove: Heat chocolate and water in heavy 1-quart saucepan on very low heat, stirring constantly until chocolate is melted and mixture is smooth. Add $^1/_2$ cup sugar; cook and stir 2 minutes. Cool to lukewarm. Continue as directed above.

Prep Time: 10 minutes
Bake Time: 40 minutes
Refrigerate Time: 3 hours

White Chocolate Pound Cake

  3 cups flour

  1 teaspoon CALUMET® baking powder

  1/2 teaspoon salt

  1 container (8 ounces) BREAKSTONE'S® *or* KNUDSEN® Sour
    Cream

  1 can (8 ounces) crushed pineapple in juice, undrained

  1 cup (2 sticks) butter, softened

  2 cups sugar

  5 eggs

  1 package (6 squares) BAKER'S® Premium White Baking
    Chocolate, melted, cooled slightly

  2 teaspoons vanilla

  1/2 cup BAKER'S® ANGEL FLAKE® Coconut

HEAT oven to 350°F. Lightly grease and flour 12-cup fluted tube pan.

MIX flour, baking powder and salt; set aside. Mix sour cream and pineapple; set aside.

BEAT butter and sugar in large bowl with electric mixer on medium speed until light and fluffy. Add eggs, 1 at a time, beating well after each addition. Beat in melted chocolate and vanilla. Add flour mixture alternately with sour cream mixture. Beat in coconut. Pour into prepared pan.

BAKE 70 to 75 minutes or until toothpick inserted near center comes out clean. Cool in pan 10 minutes on wire rack. Loosen cake from side of pan with small knife or spatula. Invert cake onto rack; gently remove pan. Cool completely on wire rack. Sprinkle with powdered sugar, if desired.

Makes 12 to 16 servings

Prep Time: 20 minutes
Bake Time: 75 minutes

White Chocolate Pound Cake

Mocha Walnut Torte

TORTE

> 5 squares BAKER'S® Semi-Sweet Baking Chocolate
>
> $^{1}/_{2}$ cup corn syrup
>
> $^{1}/_{2}$ cup (1 stick) butter *or* margarine
>
> 2 tablespoons MAXWELL HOUSE® Instant Coffee
>
> $^{3}/_{4}$ cup sugar
>
> 3 eggs
>
> 1 teaspoon vanilla
>
> 1 cup flour
>
> 1 cup chopped walnuts

GLAZE

> 3 squares BAKER'S® Semi-Sweet Baking Chocolate
>
> 1 tablespoon butter
>
> 2 tablespoons corn syrup
>
> 1 teaspoon MAXWELL HOUSE® Instant Coffee

TORTE

HEAT oven to 350°F. Lightly grease and flour 9-inch round cake pan.

MICROWAVE chocolate, corn syrup, butter and instant coffee in large microwavable bowl on HIGH 2 minutes or until the butter is melted. Stir until chocolate is completely melted.

STIR sugar into chocolate mixture until well blended. Mix in eggs and vanilla. Stir in flour and walnuts until well blended. Spread in prepared pan.

BAKE 40 to 45 minutes or until toothpick inserted in center comes out clean. DO NOT OVERBAKE. Cool cake in pan 10 minutes; remove from pan. Gently invert cake onto rack; cool completely.

GLAZE
MICROWAVE chocolate and butter in medium microwavable bowl on HIGH 1½ minutes. Stir until chocolate is completely melted. Stir in corn syrup and instant coffee until well blended. Spread glaze evenly over top and side of cake. Let stand 1 hour or until glaze is set.

Makes 8 servings

Prep Time: 15 minutes
Bake Time: 45 minutes

Make sure the utensils you use for melting chocolate are completely dry. Moisture makes the chocolate become stiff and grainy. If this happens, add ½ teaspoon shortening (not butter) for each ounce of chocolate and stir until smooth.

Baker's® One Bowl Chocolate Cake

    6 squares BAKER'S® Semi-Sweet Baking Chocolate
 ³/₄ cup (1¹/₂ sticks) butter *or* margarine
1¹/₂ cups sugar
    3 eggs
    2 teaspoons vanilla
2¹/₂ cups flour
    1 teaspoon baking soda
 ¹/₄ teaspoon salt
1¹/₂ cups water
    BAKER'S® One Bowl Chocolate Frosting (recipe follows)

HEAT oven to 350°F. Grease and flour 2 (9-inch) round cake pans.

MICROWAVE chocolate and butter in large microwavable bowl on HIGH 2 minutes or until butter is melted. Stir until chocolate is completely melted.

STIR sugar into chocolate mixture. Beat in eggs, one at a time, with electric mixer on low speed until completely mixed. Add vanilla. Stir in ¹/₂ cup of the flour, baking soda and salt. Beat in the remaining 2 cups flour alternately with water until well blended. Pour into prepared pans.

BAKE 35 minutes or until toothpick inserted into centers comes out clean. Cool 10 minutes; remove from pans. Cool completely on wire racks. Fill and frost layers with BAKER'S® One Bowl Chocolate Frosting.

Makes 12 servings

Prep Time: 15 minutes
Bake Time: 35 minutes

Baker's® One Bowl Chocolate Frosting

1 package (8 squares) BAKER'S® Semi-Sweet Baking Chocolate
1 package (16 ounces) powdered sugar (about 4 cups)
$^1/_2$ cup (1 stick) butter *or* margarine, softened
2 teaspoons vanilla
$^1/_3$ cup milk

MICROWAVE chocolate in large microwavable bowl on HIGH
2 minutes. Stir until chocolate is melted and smooth. Cool 5 minutes or
to room temperature.

ADD sugar, butter and vanilla. Gradually beat in milk with electric mixer
on low speed until well blended. If frosting becomes too thick, beat in
additional milk by teaspoonfuls until of spreading consistency.

Makes 3$^1/_4$ cups

Prep Time: 10 minutes

*Store two- or three layer cakes in a cake saver or
under a large inverted bowl. Be sure to insert a
teaspoon handle under the edge of the cover to
prevent an airtight seal and moisture buildup.*

Pleasing Pies

The aroma of a homemade pie in the oven will keep everyone at the table for dessert. Choose a favorite recipe or try them all.

Chocolate Chunk Cookie Pie

1/2 package (15 ounces) refrigerated pie crust

3/4 cup (1 1/2 sticks) butter *or* margarine, softened

1/2 cup granulated sugar

1/2 cup firmly packed brown sugar

2 eggs

1 teaspoon vanilla

1/2 cup flour

1 cup BAKER'S® Semi-Sweet Chocolate Chunks

1 cup chopped nuts (optional)

HEAT oven to 325°F. Prepare pie crust as directed on package, using 9-inch pie plate.

BEAT butter and sugars in large bowl with electric mixer on medium speed until light and fluffy. Add eggs and vanilla; beat well. Beat in flour on low speed. Stir in chocolate chunks and nuts. Spread in prepared crust.

BAKE 65 to 70 minutes or until toothpick inserted into center comes out clean. Cool completely on wire rack. *Makes 8 servings*

Special Extra: Serve with thawed COOL WHIP® Whipped Topping or vanilla ice cream.

Prep Time: 20 minutes
Bake Time: 70 minutes

Cream Cheese Brownie Pie

$^1/_2$ package (15 ounces) refrigerated pie crust

1 package (8 ounces) PHILADELPHIA® Cream Cheese, softened

$^1/_4$ cup sugar

3 eggs, divided

6 squares BAKER'S® Semi-Sweet Baking Chocolate

$^1/_2$ cup (1 stick) butter *or* margarine

$^2/_3$ cup sugar

1 teaspoon vanilla

1 cup flour

2 squares BAKER'S® Semi-Sweet Baking Chocolate, melted
(optional)

HEAT oven to 350°F. Prepare crust as directed on package, using 9-inch pie plate. Mix cream cheese, $^1/_4$ cup sugar and 1 egg in medium bowl until well blended; set aside.

MICROWAVE chocolate and butter in large microwavable bowl on HIGH 2 minutes or until butter is melted. Stir until chocolate is completely melted.

STIR $^2/_3$ cup sugar into chocolate mixture until well blended. Mix in 2 eggs and vanilla. Stir in flour until well blended. Spread half of the brownie batter into prepared crust. Carefully spread cream cheese mixture over top. Top with remaining brownie batter.

BAKE 45 minutes or until toothpick inserted in center comes out with fudgy crumbs. Cool completely on wire rack. Drizzle with melted chocolate, if desired.   *Makes 10 servings*

To soften cream cheese in the microwave: Place 1 completely unwrapped (8-ounce) package of cream cheese in microwavable bowl. Microwave on HIGH 15 seconds. Add 15 seconds for each additional package of cream cheese.

Prep Time: 30 minutes
Bake Time: 45 minutes

Semi-sweet baking chocolate is pure chocolate combined with sugar and extra cocoa butter. It is sold in a variety of forms, including one-ounce squares, bars, chips and chunks. It is interchangeable with bittersweet chocolate in most recipes.

White Chocolate Coconut Cream Pie

COCONUT CRUST

    1 cup BAKER'S® ANGEL FLAKE® Coconut

    5 tablespoons butter *or* margarine, divided

    $1/2$ cup HONEY MAID® Graham Cracker Crumbs

    3 squares BAKER'S® Premium White Baking Chocolate

COCONUT CREAM FILLING

    $1^{3}/4$ cups half-and-half

    1 package (4-serving size) JELL-O® Coconut Cream Flavor
        Instant Pudding & Pie Filling

    $1/2$ cup BAKER'S® ANGEL FLAKE® Coconut

WHITE CHOCOLATE TOPPING

    3 squares BAKER'S® Premium White Baking Chocolate

    $1^{1}/2$ cups whipping (heavy) cream, divided

COCONUT CRUST

HEAT oven to 350°F. Mix coconut, 4 tablespoons of melted butter and crumbs in 9-inch pie plate until well blended. Press onto bottom and up side of pie plate. Bake 10 minutes. Microwave chocolate and remaining 1 tablespoon butter in small microwavable bowl on HIGH $1^{1}/2$ minutes or until butter is melted. Stir until chocolate is completely melted. Spread onto bottom of prepared crust. Refrigerate 15 minutes or until chocolate is firm.

continued on page 40

White Chocolate Coconut Cream Pie

White Chocolate Coconut Cream Pie, continued

COCONUT CREAM FILLING

POUR half-and-half into large bowl. Add pudding mix and coconut. Beat with wire whisk 2 minutes. Spoon into crust. Refrigerate until ready to top.

WHITE CHOCOLATE TOPPING

MICROWAVE chocolate and ¼ cup of the cream in large microwavable bowl on HIGH 2 minutes. Stir until chocolate is completely melted. Cool 20 minutes or until room temperature, stirring occasionally.

BEAT remaining 1¼ cups cream in chilled large bowl with electric mixer on medium-high speed until medium peaks form. Fold ½ of the whipped cream into chocolate mixture. Fold in remaining whipped cream just until blended. Spoon over filling.

REFRIGERATE 4 hours or until ready to serve.   *Makes 8 servings*

Special Extra: Garnish with toasted BAKER'S® ANGEL FLAKE® Coconut.

Prep Time: 45 minutes
Refrigerate Time: 4 hours

German's® Sweet Chocolate Pie

  1 package (4 ounces) BAKER'S® GERMAN'S® Sweet Chocolate
  1/2 cup milk, divided
  4 ounces (1/2 of 8-ounce package) PHILADELPHIA® Cream
      Cheese, softened
  2 tablespoons sugar
  1 tub (8 ounces) COOL WHIP® Whipped Topping, thawed
  1 HONEY MAID® Graham Pie Crust (6 ounces or 9 inch)

MICROWAVE chocolate and 2 tablespoons of the milk in large microwavable bowl on HIGH 2 minutes. Stir until chocolate is completely melted.

BEAT in cream cheese, sugar and remaining milk with wire whisk until well blended. Refrigerate about 10 minutes to cool. Gently stir in whipped topping until smooth. Spoon into crust.

FREEZE 4 hours or until firm. Garnish with additional whipped topping and toasted coconut, if desired. Let stand at room temperature about 15 minutes or until pie can be cut easily.   *Makes 8 servings*

Special Extra: To prepare Coconut Crust, mix 1 package (7 ounces) BAKER'S® ANGEL FLAKE® Coconut (2 2/3 cups) and 1/3 cup butter *or* margarine, melted, in 9-inch pie plate. Press onto bottom and up side of pie plate. Bake in preheated 350°F oven for 20 to 30 minutes or until golden brown. Cool on wire rack. Continue as directed.

Prep Time: 20 minutes
Freeze Time: 4 hours

Raspberry Ganache Pie

1 package (8 squares) BAKER'S® Semi-Sweet Baking Chocolate,
    broken in half
1 cup whipping (heavy) cream
6 tablespoons seedless raspberry jam, divided
1 OREO® Pie Crust (9 inch)
2 cups raspberries
1 tablespoon water

PLACE chocolate in medium bowl; set aside. Mix cream and
2 tablespoons of the jam in small saucepan. Bring to gentle boil, stirring
constantly. Remove from heat. Pour over chocolate in bowl. Let stand
2 minutes.

WHISK until chocolate is melted and mixture is smooth. Pour into crust;
cover. Refrigerate 4 hours or overnight.

ARRANGE raspberries on top of pie. Microwave remaining $1/4$ cup jam
and water in small microwavable bowl on HIGH 30 seconds. Stir until
smooth. Brush over raspberries. Refrigerate until ready to serve.

Makes 12 servings

Make-Ahead: Pie can be prepared, covered and frozen. Thaw in
refrigerator for 2 hours before serving.

Prep Time: 15 minutes
Refrigerate Time: 4 hours

Clockwise from top left: Chocolate Truffle Loaf (page 92), Raspberry Truffle Brownies (page 78) and Raspberry Ganache Pie

Walnut Fudge Pie

$^1/_2$ package (15 ounces) refrigerated pie crust

1 package (8 squares) BAKER'S® Semi-Sweet Baking Chocolate

$^1/_4$ cup ($^1/_2$ stick) butter *or* margarine, softened

$^3/_4$ cup firmly packed brown sugar

3 eggs

1 teaspoon vanilla

$^1/_4$ cup flour

1 cup chopped walnuts

$^1/_2$ cup walnut halves *or* pieces

HEAT oven to 375°F. Prepare pie crust as directed on package, using 9-inch pie plate.

MICROWAVE chocolate in large microwavable bowl on HIGH 2 minutes. Stir until completely melted.

BEAT butter and sugar in large bowl with electric mixer on medium speed until light and fluffy. Add eggs, 1 at a time, beating well after each addition. Stir in melted chocolate and vanilla until blended. Stir in flour and chopped walnuts. Pour into prepared crust. Arrange walnut halves on filling.

BAKE in lower third of oven for 25 minutes or until set. Cool completely on wire rack. Refrigerate at least 1 hour or until ready to serve.

Makes 10 to 12 servings

Prep Time: 20 minutes
Bake Time: 25 minutes
Refrigerate Time: 1 hour

Chocolate Mousse Pie

12 squares (1$^1/_2$ packages) BAKER'S® Semi-Sweet Baking
    Chocolate
2 cups whipping (heavy) cream, divided
2 teaspoons powdered sugar
1 teaspoon vanilla
1 OREO® Pie Crust (9 inch)

MICROWAVE chocolate and $^3/_4$ cup of the cream in large microwavable
bowl on HIGH 2 minutes. Stir until chocolate is completely melted. Cool
20 minutes or until room temperature, stirring occasionally.

BEAT remaining 1$^1/_4$ cups cream, sugar and vanilla in chilled large bowl
with electric mixer on medium speed until medium peaks form. Fold $^1/_2$ of
the whipped cream into chocolate mixture. Fold in remaining whipped
cream just until blended. Spoon into crust.

REFRIGERATE 4 hours or until ready to serve.   *Makes 8 servings*

Special Extra: Garnish with grated BAKER'S® Semi-Sweet Baking
Chocolate.

Prep Time: 20 minutes
Refrigerate Time: 4 hours

Chocolate Pecan Pie

$^1/_2$ package (15 ounces) refrigerated pie crust

1 package (8 squares) BAKER'S® Semi-Sweet Baking Chocolate, divided

2 tablespoons butter *or* margarine

3 eggs, lightly beaten

1 cup corn syrup

$^1/_4$ cup firmly packed light brown sugar

1 teaspoon vanilla

1 $^1/_2$ cups pecan halves *or* walnut pieces

HEAT oven to 350°F. Prepare pie crust as directed on package, using 9-inch pie plate. Coarsely chop 4 squares of the chocolate; set aside.

MICROWAVE remaining 4 squares of chocolate and butter in large microwavable bowl on HIGH 2 minutes or until butter is melted. Stir until chocolate is completely melted.

BRUSH bottom of pie crust with small amount of beaten eggs. Stir remaining eggs, corn syrup, sugar and vanilla into chocolate mixture until well blended. Stir in pecans and chopped chocolate. Pour into crust.

BAKE 55 minutes or until knife inserted 2 inches from edge comes out clean. Cool completely on wire rack.   *Makes 8 servings*

Note: A frozen deep-dish pie crust (9-inch) can be substituted for the refrigerated pie crust.

Prep Time: 15 minutes
Bake Time: 55 minutes

Chocolate Pecan Pie

Mocha Truffle Pie

1 package (8 squares) BAKER'S® Semi-Sweet Baking Chocolate,
    broken in half
1 cup whipping (heavy) cream
$^1/_4$ cup plus 2 tablespoons GENERAL FOODS
    INTERNATIONAL COFFEES®, any flavor, divided
2 tablespoons sugar
1 teaspoon vanilla
1 OREO® Pie Crust *or* HONEY MAID® Graham Pie Crust
    (6 ounces or 9 inch)
1 tub (8 ounces) COOL WHIP® Whipped Topping, thawed

PLACE chocolate in medium bowl; set aside. Mix cream, $^1/_4$ cup of the flavored instant coffee and sugar in small saucepan. Bring to gentle boil, stirring constantly. Remove from heat. Pour over chocolate in bowl. Let stand 2 minutes.

WHISK until chocolate is melted and mixture is smooth. Whisk in vanilla. Pour into crust; cover. Refrigerate 4 hours or overnight.

STIR remaining 2 tablespoons flavored instant coffee into whipped topping in tub until blended. Spread over top of pie. Refrigerate until ready to serve. *Makes 12 servings*

Make-Ahead: Pie can be prepared, covered and frozen. Thaw in refrigerator for 2 hours before serving.

Prep Time: 15 minutes
Refrigerate Time: 4 hours

Decadent Pie

$^1/_2$ package (15 ounces) refrigerated pie crust

$^3/_4$ cup firmly packed brown sugar

$^3/_4$ cup light *or* dark corn syrup

4 squares BAKER'S® Semi-Sweet Baking Chocolate

6 tablespoons butter *or* margarine

3 eggs

$1^1/_3$ cups ($3^1/_2$ ounces) BAKER'S® ANGEL FLAKE® Coconut

1 cup chopped pecans

1 tub (8 ounces) COOL WHIP® Whipped Topping, thawed

HEAT oven to 350°F. Prepare pie crust as directed on package, using 9-inch pie plate.

MICROWAVE brown sugar and corn syrup in large microwavable bowl on HIGH 3 minutes or until boiling. Stir in chocolate and butter until chocolate is completely melted. Cool slightly.

STIR in eggs, 1 at a time, beating well after each addition. Stir in coconut and pecans. Pour into prepared crust.

BAKE 1 hour or until pie is set. Cool completely on wire rack. Top with whipped topping before serving.   *Makes 8 servings*

Note: A frozen deep-dish pie crust (9-inch) can be substituted for the refrigerated pie crust.

Prep Time: 15 minutes
Bake Time: 1 hour

Awesome Sundae Pie

6 squares BAKER'S® Semi-Sweet Baking Chocolate

1 tablespoon butter *or* margarine

¾ cup finely chopped nuts, toasted

¾ cup BAKER'S® ANGEL FLAKE® Coconut

2 pints ice cream, any flavor, softened

Thawed COOL WHIP® Whipped Topping, chopped nuts and maraschino cherries

Hot Fudge Sauce (recipe page 52)

LINE 9-inch pie plate with foil; lightly grease foil.

MICROWAVE chocolate and butter in large microwavable bowl on HIGH 2 minutes or until butter is melted. Stir until chocolate is completely melted. Stir in nuts and coconut. Spread evenly onto bottom and up side of prepared pie plate.

REFRIGERATE 1 hour or until firm. Lift crust out of pie plate. Carefully peel off foil. Return crust to pie plate or place on serving plate. Refrigerate until ready to use. Fill crust with scoops of ice cream and cover.

FREEZE 2 hours or until firm. Garnish with whipped topping, nuts and maraschino cherries. Serve with Hot Fudge Sauce.   *Makes 8 servings*

Tip: To serve pie, let stand at room temperature 10 minutes or until pie can be easily cut.

Prep Time: 20 minutes
Refrigerate Time: 1 hour
Freeze Time: 2 hours

continued on page 52

Awesome Sundae Pie

Awesome Sundae Pie, continued

Hot Fudge Sauce

1 package (8 squares) BAKER'S® Unsweetened Baking Chocolate
1/4 cup (1/2 stick) butter *or* margarine
1/2 cup milk
1/2 cup whipping (heavy) cream
2 cups sugar
1 tablespoon vanilla

MICROWAVE chocolate and butter in large microwavable bowl on HIGH 2 minutes or until butter is melted. Stir until chocolate is completely melted.

STIR in milk, cream and sugar until well blended. Microwave 5 minutes until mixture is thick and smooth and sugar is completely dissolved, stirring halfway through cooking time. Stir in vanilla. Pour into clean canning jars. Store in refrigerator up to 2 weeks. Before giving, attach warming directions (see below) to jar.   *Makes 3 1/2 cups*

Warming Directions: Microwave, uncovered, on HIGH 2 minutes or just until heated through.

Prep Time: 10 minutes

Amazing White Chocolate Coconut Custard Pie

    3 squares BAKER'S® Premium White Baking Chocolate, melted
    2 cups milk
    $^1/_2$ cup sugar
    $^1/_2$ cup buttermilk baking mix
    4 eggs
    $^1/_4$ cup ($^1/_2$ stick) butter *or* margarine, softened
    2 teaspoons vanilla
    1$^1/_3$ cups BAKER'S® ANGEL FLAKE® Coconut (3$^1/_2$ ounces)

HEAT oven to 350°F. Grease 9-inch pie plate.

PLACE melted chocolate, milk, sugar, baking mix, eggs, butter and vanilla in blender container; cover. Blend on low speed 3 minutes.

POUR into prepared pie plate. Sprinkle with coconut.

BAKE in lower third of oven for 45 minutes or until pie is set and top is golden brown. Cool completely on wire rack.   *Makes 8 servings*

Prep Time: 10 minutes
Bake Time: 45 minutes

Brownie Bottom Pudding Pie

    4 squares BAKER'S® Semi-Sweet Baking Chocolate
 $^{1}/_{4}$ cup ($^{1}/_{2}$ stick) butter *or* margarine
 $^{3}/_{4}$ cup sugar
    2 eggs
    1 teaspoon vanilla
 $^{1}/_{2}$ cup flour
 $^{1}/_{2}$ cup chopped nuts (optional)
 $2^{1}/_{2}$ cups cold milk
    2 packages (4-serving size each) JELL-O® Chocolate Flavor Instant
       Pudding & Pie Filling
    1 tub (8 ounces) COOL WHIP® Whipped Topping, thawed
       Grated BAKER'S® Semi-Sweet Baking Chocolate

HEAT oven to 350°F. Grease 9-inch pie plate.

MICROWAVE chocolate and butter in large microwavable bowl on HIGH
2 minutes or until butter is melted. Stir until chocolate is completely melted.

STIR in sugar, eggs and vanilla until well blended. Stir in flour, then nuts.
Spread batter into prepared pie plate.

BAKE 25 minutes or until toothpick inserted in center comes out with
fudgy crumbs. DO NOT OVERBAKE. Cool completely on wire rack.

POUR milk into large bowl. Add pudding mixes. Beat with wire whisk
2 minutes. Let stand 2 minutes. Spread over brownie pie. Top with whipped
topping, then sprinkle with grated chocolate. Refrigerate until ready to serve.

Makes 8 to 10 servings

Prep Time: 20 minutes
Bake Time: 25 minutes

Top to bottom: Cream Cheese Brownie Pie (page 36) and Brownie Bottom Pudding Pie

Cookie Jar Favorites

Packed with chocolate, nuts, peanut butter or coconut, cookies are everyone's favorite snack dessert. It will be impossible to keep hands out of the cookie jar.

Peanut Butter Chocolate Chunk Cookies

1 3/4 cups flour
3/4 teaspoon baking soda
1/4 teaspoon salt
3/4 cup (1 1/2 sticks) butter *or* margarine, softened
1 cup peanut butter
1/2 cup granulated sugar
1/2 cup firmly packed brown sugar
1 egg
1 teaspoon vanilla
1 package (12 ounces) BAKER'S® Semi-Sweet Chocolate Chunks
1 cup chopped peanuts (optional)

HEAT oven to 375°F.

MIX flour, baking soda and salt in medium bowl; set aside.

BEAT butter, peanut butter and sugars in large bowl with electric mixer on medium speed until light and fluffy. Add egg and vanilla; beat well. Gradually beat in flour mixture. Stir in chocolate chunks and peanuts. Drop by heaping tablespoonfuls onto ungreased cookie sheets.

BAKE 11 to 13 minutes or just until golden brown. Cool on cookie sheets 1 minute. Remove to wire racks and cool completely.

Makes about 3 dozen cookies

Storage Know-How: Store in tightly covered container up to 1 week.

Prep Time: 15 minutes
Bake Time: 11 to 13 minutes

Death By Chocolate Cookies

2 packages (8 squares each) BAKER'S® Semi-Sweet Baking
Chocolate, divided
$^3/_4$ cup firmly packed brown sugar
$^1/_4$ cup ($^1/_2$ stick) butter *or* margarine
2 eggs
1 teaspoon vanilla
$^1/_2$ cup flour
$^1/_4$ teaspoon CALUMET® Baking Powder
2 cups chopped nuts (optional)

HEAT oven to 350°F. Coarsely chop 8 squares (1 package) of the
chocolate; set aside.

MICROWAVE remaining 8 squares chocolate in large microwavable bowl
on HIGH 2 minutes. Stir until chocolate is melted and smooth. Stir in
sugar, butter, eggs and vanilla with wooden spoon until well blended. Stir
in flour and baking powder. Stir in reserved chopped chocolate and nuts.
Drop by scant $^1/_4$ cupfuls onto ungreased cookie sheets.

BAKE 13 to 14 minutes or until cookies are puffed and feel set to the
touch. Cool on cookie sheet 1 minute. Remove to wire racks and cool
completely.   *Makes about 18 large cookies*

Note: If omitting nuts, increase flour to $^3/_4$ cup to prevent spreading.
Makes about 15 large cookies.

Death By Chocolate Cookies

Coconut Chocolate Jumbles

$^1/_2$ cup (1 stick) butter *or* margarine, softened

$^1/_2$ cup granulated sugar

$^1/_4$ cup firmly packed brown sugar

1 egg

$^1/_2$ teaspoon vanilla

1 cup flour

1 teaspoon baking soda

6 squares BAKER'S® Semi-Sweet Baking Chocolate *or* 1 package
(6 squares) BAKER'S® Premium White Baking Chocolate,
chopped

1 package (7 ounces) BAKER'S® ANGEL FLAKE® Coconut
($2^2/_3$ cups)

1 cup chopped walnuts, toasted

1 cup raisins

HEAT oven to 350°F.

BEAT butter and sugars in large bowl with electric mixer on medium
speed until light and fluffy. Add egg and vanilla; beat well. Mix in flour
and baking soda. Stir in chocolate, coconut, walnuts and raisins. Drop by
rounded tablespoonfuls, $1^1/_2$ inches apart, onto ungreased cookie sheets.

BAKE 10 to 12 minutes or until golden brown. Cool on cookie sheets
2 minutes. Remove to wire racks and cool completely.

Makes about 3 dozen cookies

Storage Know-How: Store in tightly covered container up to 1 week.

Prep Time: 15 minutes
Bake Time: 10 to 12 minutes

Double Chocolate Chunk Cookies

1 package (12 ounces) BAKER'S® Semi-Sweet Chocolate Chunks, divided
1 cup flour
$^1/_2$ teaspoon CALUMET® Baking Powder
$^1/_4$ teaspoon salt
$^1/_2$ cup (1 stick) butter *or* margarine, softened
$^1/_2$ cup firmly packed brown sugar
1 egg
1 teaspoon vanilla
1 cup chopped nuts (optional)

HEAT oven to 375°F.

MICROWAVE 1 cup of the chocolate chunks in microwavable bowl on HIGH 2 minutes until almost melted. Stir until chocolate is completely melted; set aside. Mix flour, baking powder and salt in medium bowl; set aside.

BEAT butter and sugar in large bowl with electric mixer on medium speed until light and fluffy. Add egg and vanilla; beat well. Stir in melted chocolate. Gradually beat in flour mixture. Stir in chocolate chunks and nuts. Drop by heaping tablespoonfuls onto ungreased cookie sheets.

BAKE 10 minutes or until cookies are puffed and feel set to the touch. Cool on cookie sheets 1 minute. Remove to wire racks and cool completely.   *Makes about 2 dozen cookies*

Prep Time: 15 minutes
Bake Time: 10 minutes

Tropical Chunk Cookies

 1 package (12 ounces) BAKER'S® White Chocolate Chunks, divided
1 3/4 cups flour
1 1/2 cups BAKER'S® ANGEL FLAKE® Coconut, toasted
 3/4 teaspoon baking soda
 1/4 teaspoon salt
 1/2 cup (1 stick) butter *or* margarine, softened
 1/3 cup firmly packed brown sugar
 1 egg
 1 teaspoon vanilla
 1 cup chopped macadamia nuts

HEAT oven to 375°F.

MICROWAVE 1 cup of the chocolate chunks in microwavable bowl on HIGH 2 minutes until almost melted. Stir until chocolate is completely melted; cool slightly. Mix flour, coconut, baking soda and salt in medium bowl; set aside.

BEAT butter and sugar in large bowl with electric mixer on medium speed until light and fluffy. Add egg and vanilla; beat well. Stir in melted chocolate. Gradually beat in flour mixture. Stir in remaining chocolate chunks and nuts. Drop by heaping tablespoonfuls onto ungreased cookie sheets.

BAKE 11 to 13 minutes or just until golden brown. Cool on cookie sheets 1 minute. Remove to wire racks and cool completely.

Makes about 3 dozen cookies

Prep Time: 15 minutes
Bake Time: 11 to 13 minutes

62

Tropical Chunk Cookies

Baker's® Premium Chocolate Chunk Cookies

1 ^{3}/$_4$ cups flour

^{3}/$_4$ teaspoon baking soda

^{1}/$_4$ teaspoon salt

^{3}/$_4$ cup (1 ^{1}/$_2$ sticks) butter *or* margarine, softened

^{1}/$_2$ cup granulated sugar

^{1}/$_2$ cup firmly packed brown sugar

1 egg

1 teaspoon vanilla

1 package (12 ounces) BAKER'S® Semi-Sweet Chocolate Chunks

1 cup chopped nuts (optional)

HEAT oven to 375°F.

MIX flour, baking soda and salt in medium bowl; set aside.

BEAT butter and sugars in large bowl with electric mixer on medium speed until light and fluffy. Add egg and vanilla; beat well. Gradually beat in flour mixture. Stir in chocolate chunks and nuts. Drop by heaping tablepoonfuls onto ungreased cookie sheets.

BAKE 11 to 13 minutes or just until golden brown. Cool on cookie sheets 1 minute. Remove to wire racks and cool completely.

Makes about 3 dozen cookies

continued on page 66

Prep Time: 15 minutes
Bake Time: 11 to 13 minutes

Baker's® Premium Chocolate Chunk Cookies

Baker's® Premium Chocolate Chunk Cookies, continued

Bar Cookies: Spread dough in greased foil-lined 15×10×1-inch baking pan. Bake at 375°F for 18 to 20 minutes or until golden brown. (Or, bake in 13×9-inch pan for 20 to 22 minutes.) Cool completely in pan on wire rack. Makes 3 dozen bars.

Chocolate Chunkoholic Cookies: Omit nuts. Stir in 2 packages (12 ounces each) BAKER'S® Semi-Sweet Chocolate Chunks. Drop by scant ¼ cupfuls onto cookie sheets. Bake at 375°F for 12 to 14 minutes. Makes about 22 large cookies.

To freeze cookie dough, place heaping tablespoonfuls of cookie dough on cookie sheet. Place in freezer for 1 hour. Transfer to airtight plastic container or freezer zipper-style plastic bag. Freeze dough up to 1 month. Bake frozen cookie dough at 375°F for 15 to 16 minutes or just until golden brown.

Mocha Melt Cookies

4 squares BAKER'S® Unsweetened Baking Chocolate

$1/2$ cup (1 stick) butter *or* margarine, softened

$1^1/4$ cups sugar

1 egg

1 teaspoon vanilla

$1/3$ cup milk

$1^1/4$ cups flour

$1/2$ cup GENERAL FOODS INTERNATIONAL COFFEES®,
     any flavor

2 teaspoons CALUMET® Baking Powder

HEAT oven to 350°F.

MICROWAVE chocolate in large microwavable bowl on HIGH $1^1/2$ minutes or until almost melted. Stir until chocolate is completely melted.

BEAT in butter and sugar with electric mixer on medium speed until well blended. Add egg and vanilla; beat well. Blend in milk. Beat in flour, flavored instant coffee and baking powder on low speed. Drop by tablespoonfuls, 2 inches apart, onto ungreased cookie sheets.

BAKE 9 minutes or until cookies are puffed and a slight indentation remains when touched lightly. Cool on cookie sheets 2 minutes. Remove to wire racks and cool completely.   *Makes about 3 dozen cookies*

Storage Know-How: Store in tightly covered container up to 1 week.

Prep Time: 15 minutes
Bake Time: 9 minutes

Super Chunk Oatmeal Cookie Mix

    1 cup sugar

    1 teaspoon cinnamon

    1 cup flour

    $^1/_2$ teaspoon baking soda

    $^1/_4$ teaspoon salt

    1 cup quick-cooking rolled oats

    1 package (12 ounces) BAKER'S® Semi-Sweet Chocolate Chunks, divided

    $^1/_2$ cup chopped nuts

LAYER ingredients in $1^1/_2$-quart glass canister or jar in the following order: sugar mixed with cinnamon, flour, baking soda, salt, oats, chocolate chunks and nuts. Tap jar gently on counter to settle each layer before adding next one. Cover.

ATTACH baking directions (see below) to jar.

BAKING DIRECTIONS

HEAT oven to 375°F. Beat $^3/_4$ cup ($1^1/_2$ sticks) softened butter, 1 egg and 1 teaspoon vanilla in large bowl with electric mixer on medium speed until well blended. Empty contents of jar into bowl. Stir until well mixed. Drop by heaping tablespoonfuls onto ungreased cookie sheets.

BAKE 12 to 13 minutes or until golden brown. Cool on cookie sheets 1 minute. Remove to wire racks and cool completely.

Makes about 3 dozen cookies

Prep Time: 10 minutes

Super Chunk Oatmeal Cookie Mix

Chocolate White Chocolate Chunk Cookies

2 cups flour
2 teaspoons CALUMET® Baking Powder
$^1/_4$ teaspoon salt
$^3/_4$ cup (1 $^1/_2$ sticks) butter *or* margarine, softened
1 $^1/_2$ cups firmly packed brown sugar
2 eggs
1 teaspoon vanilla
4 squares BAKER'S® Unsweetened Baking Chocolate, melted, cooled slightly
1 package (12 ounces) BAKER'S® White Chocolate Chunks
1 cup chopped nuts (optional)

HEAT oven to 350°F.

MIX flour, baking powder and salt in medium bowl; set aside.

BEAT butter and sugar in large bowl with electric mixer on medium speed until light and fluffy. Add eggs and vanilla; beat well. Stir in melted chocolate. Gradually beat in flour mixture. Stir in chocolate chunks and nuts. Drop by heaping tablespoonfuls onto ungreased cookie sheets.

BAKE 11 to 12 minutes or until cookies feel set to the touch. Cool on cookie sheets 1 minute. Remove to wire racks and cool completely.

Makes about 3$^1/_2$ dozen cookies

Storage Know-How: Store in tightly covered container up to 1 week.

Make-Ahead: After cookies are completely cooled, wrap in plastic wrap and place in an airtight plastic container or zipper-style plastic freezer bag. Cookies can be frozen for up to 1 month. Bring cookies to room temperature before serving.

Prep Time: 15 minutes
Bake Time: 11 to 12 minutes

Chocolate White Chocolate Chunk Cookies

Easy Chocolate Macaroons

2 squares BAKER'S® Unsweetened Baking Chocolate
1 can (15 ounces) sweetened condensed milk
2 squares BAKER'S® Premium White Baking Chocolate, chopped
2 cups BAKER'S® ANGEL FLAKE® Coconut
1 cup chopped pecans

HEAT oven to 350°F.

MICROWAVE unsweetened chocolate and condensed milk in large microwavable bowl on HIGH 2 minutes or until chocolate is almost melted. Stir until chocolate is completely melted.

STIR in chopped white chocolate, coconut and pecans. Drop by heaping teaspoonfuls onto greased cookie sheets.

BAKE 10 to 12 minutes or until tops are set. Immediately remove to wire racks and cool completely.   *Makes about 2 dozen cookies*

Storage Know-How: Store in tightly covered container up to 1 week.

Prep Time: 15 minutes
Bake Time: 10 to 12 minutes

Chocolate Brownie Cookies

6 squares BAKER'S® Semi-Sweet Baking Chocolate *or* 1 package
 (6 squares) BAKER'S® Bittersweet Baking Chocolate

4 squares BAKER'S® Unsweetened Baking Chocolate

6 tablespoons butter *or* margarine

1 1/4 cups sugar

3 eggs, lightly beaten

2 teaspoons vanilla

1 cup flour

1 teaspoon CALUMET® Baking Powder

1/4 teaspoon salt

2 cups toasted chopped walnuts (optional)

HEAT oven to 325°F.

MICROWAVE semi-sweet chocolate, unsweetened chocolate and butter
in large microwavable bowl on HIGH 2 minutes or until butter is melted.
Stir until chocolate is completely melted.

STIR sugar into chocolate mixture until blended. Mix in eggs and vanilla.
Stir in flour, baking powder and salt. Stir in nuts. Drop by rounded
tablespoonfuls, 1 1/2 inches apart, onto ungreased cookie sheets.

BAKE 12 minutes or until set. DO NOT OVERBAKE. Cool on cookie
sheets 5 minutes. Remove to wire racks and cool completely.

Makes about 3 dozen cookies

Storage Know-How: Store in tightly covered container up to 1 week.

Prep Time: 15 minutes
Bake Time: 12 minutes

Chocolate Sugar Cookies

    2 cups flour
    1 teaspoon baking soda
    1/4 teaspoon salt
    3 squares BAKER'S® Unsweetened Baking Chocolate
    1 cup (2 sticks) butter *or* margarine
    1 cup sugar
    1 egg
    1 teaspoon vanilla
       Additional sugar

HEAT oven to 375°F. Mix flour, baking soda and salt in medium bowl; set aside.

MICROWAVE chocolate and butter in large microwavable bowl on HIGH 2 minutes or until butter is melted. Stir until chocolate is completely melted.

STIR sugar into chocolate mixture until well blended. Mix in egg and vanilla. Stir in flour mixture until well blended. Refrigerate dough about 15 minutes or until easy to handle.

SHAPE dough into 1-inch balls; roll in additional sugar. Place on ungreased cookie sheets.

BAKE 8 to 10 minutes. (If a flatter, crisper cookie is desired, flatten with bottom of glass before baking.) Cool on cookie sheets 1 minute. Remove to wire racks and cool completely.   *Makes about 3 1/2 dozen cookies*

Jam-Filled Chocolate Sugar Cookies: Prepare dough as directed. Roll in finely chopped nuts in place of sugar. Make indentation in each ball; fill center with your favorite jam. Bake as directed.

Chocolate-Caramel Sugar Cookies: Prepare dough as directed. Roll in finely chopped nuts in place of sugar. Make indentation in each ball; bake as directed. Microwave 1 package (14 ounces) caramels and 2 tablespoons milk in microwavable bowl on HIGH 3 minutes or until melted, stirring after 2 minutes. Fill centers of cookies with caramel mixture. Drizzle with melted BAKER'S® Semi-Sweet Baking Chocolate.

Prep Time: 20 minutes
Bake Time: 10 minutes

Chocolate Sugar Cookies

Scrumptious Brownies & Bars

With their irresistible rich chocolate
flavor, brownies and bars make great
snacks—and they're perfect anytime
you need to satisfy a chocolate craving.

Baker's® One Bowl Brownies

4 squares BAKER'S® Unsweetened Baking Chocolate

¾ cup (1½ sticks) butter *or* margarine

2 cups sugar

3 eggs

1 teaspoon vanilla

1 cup flour

1 cup coarsely chopped nuts (optional)

HEAT oven to 350°F. Line 13×9-inch baking pan with foil; grease foil.

MICROWAVE chocolate and butter in large microwavable bowl on HIGH 2 minutes or until butter is melted. Stir until chocolate is completely melted.

STIR sugar into chocolate mixture until well blended. Mix in eggs and vanilla. Stir in flour and nuts until well blended. Spread in prepared pan.

BAKE 30 to 35 minutes or until toothpick inserted into center comes out with fudgy crumbs. DO NOT OVERBAKE. Cool in pan on wire rack. Lift out of pan onto cutting board.   *Makes 2 dozen brownies*

Tips: For cakelike brownies, stir in ½ cup milk with eggs and vanilla and increase flour to 1½ cups. For extra fudgy brownies, use 4 eggs. For extra thick brownies, bake in 9-inch square baking pan 50 minutes. For 13×9-inch glass baking dish, bake at 325°F.

Prep Time: 15 minutes
Bake Time: 35 minutes

Raspberry Truffle Brownies

BROWNIES

4 squares BAKER'S® Unsweetened Baking Chocolate

$^3/_4$ cup (1$^1/_2$ sticks) butter *or* margarine

2 cups sugar

3 eggs

1 teaspoon vanilla

1 cup flour

1 cup coarsely chopped macadamia nuts *or* toasted, slivered almonds

$^1/_4$ cup seedless raspberry jam

GLAZE

1 cup whipping (heavy) cream

6 squares BAKER'S® Semi-Sweet Baking Chocolate, finely chopped

2 squares BAKER'S® Unsweetened Baking Chocolate, finely chopped

3 tablespoons seedless raspberry jam

BROWNIES

HEAT oven to 350°F. Line 13×9-inch baking pan with foil; grease foil.

MICROWAVE chocolate and butter in large microwavable bowl on HIGH 2 minutes or until butter is melted. Stir until chocolate is completely melted.

STIR sugar into chocolate mixture until well blended. Mix in eggs and vanilla. Stir in flour and nuts until well blended. Spread in prepared pan.

BAKE 30 to 35 minutes or until toothpick inserted in center comes out with fudgy crumbs. DO NOT OVERBAKE. Cool in pan on wire rack. Spread jam over brownies.

GLAZE
MICROWAVE cream in medium microwavable bowl on HIGH 1 minute or until simmering. Stir in chopped chocolates and jam until chocolates are melted and mixture is smooth. Spread glaze over jam layer on brownies.

REFRIGERATE 1 hour or until glaze is set. Lift out of pan onto cutting board.   *Makes 2 dozen brownies*

Tip: For 13×9-inch glass baking dish, bake at 325°F.

Prep Time: 20 minutes
Bake Time: 35 minutes
Refrigerate Time: 1 hour

*Cut Raspberry Truffle Brownies into diamond-
shaped bars. Garnish each bar with fresh raspberry.
Makes about 3 dozen.*

Easy Cookie Bars

$^1/_2$ cup (1 stick) butter *or* margarine, melted
1$^1/_2$ cups HONEY MAID® Graham Cracker Crumbs
1$^1/_3$ cups (3$^1/_2$ ounces) BAKER'S® ANGEL FLAKE® Coconut
1 cup BAKER'S® Semi-Sweet Chocolate Chunks
1 cup chopped nuts
1 can (14 ounces) sweetened condensed milk

HEAT oven to 350°F. Line 13×9-inch baking pan with foil; grease foil.

MIX butter and graham cracker crumbs in medium bowl. Press into prepared pan. Sprinkle with coconut, chocolate chunks and nuts. Pour condensed milk over top.

BAKE 25 to 30 minutes or until golden brown. Cool in pan on wire rack. Lift out of pan onto cutting board.   *Makes 3 dozen bars*

Tip: For 13×9-inch glass baking dish, bake at 325°F.

Special Extra: Melt $^1/_2$ cup BAKER'S® Semi-Sweet Chocolate Chunks as directed on package. Drizzle over top of bars.

Prep Time: 15 minutes
Bake Time: 30 minutes

Easy Cookie Bars

Mississippi Mud Bars

$^1/_2$ cup (1 stick) butter *or* margarine

$^3/_4$ cup firmly packed brown sugar

1 egg

1 teaspoon vanilla

1 cup flour

$^1/_2$ teaspoon baking soda

$^1/_4$ teaspoon salt

1 package (8 squares) BAKER'S® Semi-Sweet Baking Chocolate, chopped, divided

1 package (6 squares) BAKER'S® Premium White Baking Chocolate, chopped, divided

1 cup chopped walnuts, divided

HEAT oven to 350°F. Line 9-inch square baking pan with foil; grease foil.

BEAT butter, sugar, egg and vanilla in large bowl with electric mixer on medium speed until light and fluffy. Mix in flour, baking soda and salt. Stir in $^1/_2$ each of the semi-sweet and white chocolates and $^1/_2$ cup of the walnuts. Spread in prepared pan.

BAKE 25 minutes or until toothpick inserted in center comes out almost clean. DO NOT OVERBAKE. Remove from oven. Sprinkle with remaining semi-sweet and white chocolates. Cover with foil. Let stand 5 minutes or until chocolates are melted. Swirl with knife to marbleize. Sprinkle with remaining $^1/_2$ cup walnuts. Cool in pan on wire rack. Lift out of pan onto cutting board. *Makes 16 bars*

Prep Time: 20 minutes
Bake Time: 25 minutes

Cream Cheese Brownies

4 squares BAKER'S® Unsweetened Baking Chocolate

$^3/_4$ cup (1 $^1/_2$ sticks) butter *or* margarine

2 $^1/_2$ cups sugar, divided

5 eggs, divided

1 $^1/_4$ cups flour, divided

1 package (8 ounces) PHILADELPHIA® Cream Cheese, softened

HEAT oven to 350°F. Line 13×9-inch baking pan with foil; grease foil.

MICROWAVE chocolate and butter in large microwavable bowl on HIGH 2 minutes or until butter is melted. Stir until chocolate is completely melted.

STIR 2 cups of the sugar into chocolate mixture until well blended. Mix in 4 of the eggs. Stir in 1 cup of the flour until well blended. Spread in prepared pan. Beat cream cheese, remaining $^1/_2$ cup sugar, 1 egg and $^1/_4$ cup flour in same bowl with wire whisk until well blended. Spoon mixture over brownie batter. Swirl batters with knife to marbleize.

BAKE 40 minutes or until toothpick inserted in center comes out with fudgy crumbs. DO NOT OVERBAKE. Cool in pan on wire rack. Lift out of pan onto cutting board. *Makes 2 dozen brownies*

Tip: For 13×9-inch glass baking dish, bake at 325°F.

Prep Time: 15 minutes
Bake Time: 40 minutes

Peanut Butter Layered Brownies

BROWNIES

4 squares BAKER'S® Unsweetened Baking Chocolate

3/4 cup (1 1/2 sticks) butter *or* margarine

2 cups granulated sugar

4 eggs

1 teaspoon vanilla

1 cup flour

PEANUT BUTTER LAYER

1 cup creamy peanut butter

1/2 cup powdered sugar

1 teaspoon vanilla

CHOCOLATE GLAZE

4 squares BAKER'S® Semi-Sweet Baking Chocolate

3 tablespoons butter *or* margarine

BROWNIES

HEAT oven to 350°F. Line 13×9-inch baking pan with foil; grease foil.

MICROWAVE chocolate and butter in large microwavable bowl on HIGH 2 minutes or until butter is melted. Stir until chocolate is completely melted. Stir sugar into chocolate mixture until well blended. Mix in eggs and vanilla. Stir in flour until well blended. Spread in prepared pan.

BAKE 30 to 35 minutes or until toothpick inserted in center comes out with fudgy crumbs. DO NOT OVERBAKE. Cool in pan on wire rack.

PEANUT BUTTER LAYER

MIX peanut butter, powdered sugar and vanilla in large bowl until well blended and smooth. Spread over brownies.

CHOCOLATE GLAZE

MICROWAVE chocolate and butter in small microwavable bowl on HIGH 2 minutes or until butter is melted. Stir until chocolate is completely melted. Spread over peanut butter layer. Refrigerate 30 minutes or until firm. Lift out of pan onto cutting board.

Makes 2 dozen brownies

Prep Time: 30 minutes
Bake Time: 35 minutes

*If using 13×9-inch glass baking dish,
bake at 325°F.*

Chocolate Chunk Caramel Pecan Brownies

4 squares BAKER'S® Unsweetened Baking Chocolate

$^3/_4$ cup (1$^1/_2$ sticks) butter *or* margarine

2 cups sugar

4 eggs

1 cup flour

1 package (14 ounces) KRAFT® Caramels, unwrapped

$^1/_3$ cup whipping (heavy) cream

2 cups pecan *or* walnut halves, divided

1 package (12 ounces) BAKER'S® Semi-Sweet Chocolate Chunks, divided

HEAT oven to 350°F. Line 13×9-inch baking pan with foil; grease foil.

MICROWAVE chocolate and butter in large microwavable bowl on HIGH 2 minutes or until butter is melted. Stir until chocolate is completely melted. Stir sugar into chocolate mixture until well blended. Mix in eggs. Stir in flour until well blended. Spread $^1/_2$ of brownie batter in prepared pan.

BAKE 25 minutes or until brownie is firm to the touch.

MEANWHILE, microwave caramels and cream in microwavable bowl on HIGH 2 minutes or until caramels begin to melt. Stir until smooth. Stir in 1 cup of pecan halves. Gently spread caramel mixture over baked brownie in pan. Sprinkle with $^1/_2$ of chocolate chunks. Pour remaining unbaked brownie batter evenly over top; sprinkle with remaining chocolate chunks and 1 cup pecan halves. (Some caramel mixture may peak through.)

BAKE an additional 30 minutes or until brownie is firm to the touch. Cool in pan on wire rack. Lift out of pan onto cutting board.

Makes 2 dozen brownies

Tip: For 13×9-inch glass baking dish, bake at 325°F.

Prep Time: 20 minutes
Bake Time: 55 minutes

Chocolate Chunk Caramel Pecan Brownies

Almond Snow Bars

4 squares BAKER'S® Premium White Baking Chocolate

1/2 cup (1 stick) butter *or* margarine

3/4 cup sugar

2 eggs

1 teaspoon almond extract

2/3 cup flour

1/2 teaspoon CALUMET® Baking Powder

1/4 teaspoon salt

3/4 cup chopped almonds

Powdered sugar

HEAT oven to 350°F. Line 9-inch square baking pan with foil; grease foil.

MICROWAVE chocolate and butter in large microwavable bowl on HIGH 2 minutes or until butter is melted. Stir until chocolate is completely melted.

STIR sugar into chocolate mixture until well blended. Mix in eggs and almond extract. Stir in flour, baking powder and salt until well blended. Stir in almonds. Spread in prepared pan.

BAKE 30 to 35 minutes or until golden brown. Cool in pan on wire rack. Sprinkle with powdered sugar. Lift out of pan onto cutting board.

Makes 16 bars

Tip: For 13×9-inch glass baking dish, bake at 325°F.

Prep Time: 15 minutes
Bake Time: 35 minutes

Chocolate Caramel Nut Bars

1 cup (2 sticks) butter *or* margarine, softened

1/2 cup firmly packed brown sugar

2 cups flour

1/4 teaspoon salt

1 package (12 ounces) BAKER'S® Semi-Sweet Chocolate Chunks

1 bag (14 ounces) caramels, unwrapped

1/3 cup whipping (heavy) cream

1 cup chopped walnuts *or* pecans

HEAT oven to 350°F.

BEAT butter and sugar in large bowl with electric mixer on medium speed until light and fluffy. Add flour and salt; beat on low speed until crumbly. Press into 15×10×1-inch baking pan.

BAKE 15 minutes or until edges are golden brown. Remove from oven. Sprinkle chocolate chunks over top. Cover with foil. Let stand 5 minutes or until chocolate is melted. Spread chocolate evenly over top.

MICROWAVE caramels and cream in microwavable bowl on HIGH 2 minutes or until caramels begin to melt. Stir in walnuts. Gently spread caramel mixture over chocolate. Cool in pan on wire rack.

Makes 3 dozen bars

Storage Know-How: Store in tightly covered container up to 1 week.

Prep Time: 20 minutes
Bake Time: 15 minutes

Delectable Desserts

When it comes to desserts—whether
pudding, mousse, soufflé or even
coffeecake—the more chocolate the
better!

Chocolate Chunk Cinnamon Coffee Cake

1 package (12 ounces) BAKER'S® Semi-Sweet Chocolate Chunks
³/₄ cup chopped nuts
2 cups sugar, divided
1¹/₂ teaspoons cinnamon
2²/₃ cups flour
1¹/₂ teaspoons baking soda
³/₄ teaspoon CALUMET® Baking Powder
¹/₂ teaspoon salt
³/₄ cup (1¹/₂ sticks) butter *or* margarine, softened
1 teaspoon vanilla
3 eggs
1¹/₂ cups BREAKSTONE'S® *or* KNUDSEN® Sour Cream

HEAT oven to 350°F. Grease 13×9-inch baking pan.

MIX chocolate, nuts, ²/₃ cup of the sugar and cinnamon; set aside. Mix flour, baking soda, baking powder and salt; set aside.

BEAT butter, remaining 1¹/₃ cups sugar and vanilla in large bowl with electric mixer on medium speed until light and fluffy. Add eggs, 1 at a time, beating well after each addition. Add flour mixture alternately with sour cream, beating after each addition until smooth. Spoon ¹/₂ of the batter into prepared pan. Top with ¹/₂ of the chocolate-nut mixture. Repeat layers.

BAKE 40 to 45 minutes or until toothpick inserted in center comes out clean. Cool in pan on wire rack.   *Makes 16 servings*

Prep Time: 30 minutes
Bake Time: 45 minutes

Chocolate Truffle Loaf

2 packages (8 squares each) BAKER'S® Semi-Sweet Baking
   Chocolate

$1/2$ cup corn syrup

$1/2$ cup (1 stick) butter *or* margarine

2 cups whipping (heavy) cream, divided

3 egg yolks, lightly beaten

$1/4$ cup powdered sugar

1 teaspoon vanilla

   Raspberry Sauce (recipe follows)

LINE 8×4-inch loaf pan with plastic wrap. Heat chocolate, corn syrup
and butter in 2-quart saucepan on medium heat until chocolate is melted,
stirring constantly. Beat $1/2$ cup of the cream and egg yolks until well
blended. Gradually stir into chocolate mixture. Cook 3 minutes, stirring
constantly. Cool to room temperature.

BEAT remaining $1^1/2$ cups cream, sugar and vanilla in medium bowl with
electric mixer on medium-high speed until soft peaks form. Fold into
chocolate mixture until no streaks remain. Pour into prepared pan.

REFRIGERATE overnight or freeze 3 hours. Unmold onto serving
plate; remove plastic wrap. Serve with Raspberry Sauce.

Makes 12 servings

Raspberry Sauce: Mix 1 package (10 ounces) frozen red raspberries in
light syrup, thawed, puréed and strained, $1/3$ cup light corn syrup and
$1/4$ cup orange-flavored liqueur (optional) in medium bowl until well
blended. Refrigerate until ready to serve. Makes $1^1/4$ cups.

Prep Time: 30 minutes plus refrigerating

Chocolate Pots de Creme

1 1/2 cups whipping (heavy) cream
4 squares BAKER'S® Semi-Sweet Baking Chocolate
3 egg yolks
2 tablespoons sugar
Boiling water

HEAT oven to 325°F. Place four 3/4-cup custard cups in 8- or 9-inch square baking pan.

HEAT cream and chocolate in medium saucepan on medium heat until just simmering, stirring constantly. Beat egg yolks and sugar in large bowl with wire whisk until well blended. Gradually whisk in hot cream mixture. Divide mixture among custard cups. Place pan in oven. Pour boiling water into pan to come halfway up sides of custard cups.

BAKE 25 to 30 minutes or until just set around edges but still soft in center. Remove cups from pan of water.

REFRIGERATE 4 hours or until ready to serve.   *Makes 4 servings*

Make-Ahead: Can be made 1 day ahead. Cover cooled custards with plastic wrap and refrigerate.

Prep Time: 20 minutes
Bake Time: 30 minutes
Refrigerate Time: 4 hours

Chocolate Soufflé

$^1/_2$ cup sugar

$^1/_4$ cup MINUTE® Tapioca

3 squares BAKER'S® Unsweetened Baking Chocolate, coarsely
     chopped

$^1/_4$ teaspoon salt

2 cups milk

$^1/_2$ teaspoon vanilla

3 eggs, separated

   Boiling water

   White Chocolate Sauce (recipe follows)

HEAT oven to 325°F.

MIX sugar, tapioca, chocolate, salt and milk in medium saucepan. Let
stand 5 minutes. Cook on medium heat, stirring constantly, until mixture
comes to full boil. Remove from heat. Stir in vanilla.

BEAT egg whites in large bowl with electric mixer on high speed until
stiff peaks form; set aside. Beat egg yolks in large bowl with electric mixer
on high speed until thick and lemon colored. Stir in tapioca mixture. Fold
in beaten egg whites. Pour into 6-cup soufflé dish or 1$^1/_2$-quart baking
dish. Place dish in large baking pan, then place in oven. Carefully pour
boiling water into pan to come 1 inch up side of soufflé dish.

BAKE 60 to 65 minutes or until firm. Serve warm with White Chocolate
Sauce.   *Makes 8 servings*

White Chocolate Sauce: Microwave 1 package (6 squares) BAKER'S®
Premium White Baking Chocolate and 1 cup whipping (heavy) cream in
large microwavable bowl on HIGH 4 minutes, stirring halfway through

heating time. Stir with wire whisk until chocolate is melted and mixture is smooth. Makes 1 1/2 cups.

Variation: Chocolate Soufflé can also be baked in 6 (1-cup) soufflé dishes. Bake 40 to 45 minutes or until firm.

Prep Time: 20 minutes
Bake Time: 65 minutes

Chocolate Soufflé

White Chocolate Mousse

1 package (6 squares) BAKER'S® Premium White Baking Chocolate
1¹/₂ cups whipping (heavy) cream, divided

MICROWAVE chocolate and ¹/₄ cup of the cream in large microwavable bowl on HIGH 2 minutes or until chocolate is almost melted, stirring halfway through heating time. Stir until chocolate is completely melted. Cool 20 minutes or until room temperature, stirring occasionally.

BEAT remaining 1¹/₄ cups cream in chilled medium bowl with electric mixer on medium speed until soft peaks form. DO NOT OVERBEAT. Fold ¹/₂ of the whipped cream into chocolate mixture. Fold in remaining whipped cream just until blended. Spoon into dessert dishes.

REFRIGERATE 2 hours or until ready to serve.

Makes 6 (¹/₂-cup) servings

Special Extra: Garnish with white chocolate curls and fresh raspberries or grated BAKER'S® Semi-Sweet Baking Chocolate.

Prep Time: 20 minutes

Chocolate Brownie Bread

4 squares BAKER'S® Unsweetened Baking Chocolate

1/2 cup (1 stick) butter *or* margarine

1 cup granulated sugar

1 cup firmly packed brown sugar

2 eggs

1 cup BREAKSTONE'S® *or* KNUDSEN® Sour Cream

1 teaspoon vanilla

1 1/2 cups flour

2 teaspoons CALUMET® Baking Powder

1/4 teaspoon baking soda

1 cup finely chopped walnuts, lightly toasted (optional)

HEAT oven to 350°F. Grease and flour 9×4-inch loaf pan.

MICROWAVE chocolate and butter in microwavable bowl on HIGH 2 minutes or until butter is melted. Stir until chocolate is completely melted.

STIR sugars into chocolate mixture until well blended. Stir in eggs, sour cream and vanilla. Stir in flour, baking powder and baking soda until well blended. Stir in walnuts. Spread in prepared pan.

BAKE 60 to 70 minutes or until toothpick inserted in center comes out clean. Cool in pan 10 minutes; remove from pan. Cool completely on wire rack.   *Makes 1 loaf*

Make Ahead for Gift-Giving: After bread is completely cooled, wrap in plastic wrap and place in freezer-weight zipper-style plastic bag. Bread can be frozen for up to 1 month.

Prep Time: 15 minutes
Bake Time: 70 minutes

Chocolate Dipped Delights

2 packages (4 ounces each) BAKER'S® GERMAN'S® Sweet
   Chocolate *or* 1 package (8 ounces) BAKER'S® Semi-Sweet
   Baking Chocolate
   Assorted dippers such as whole strawberries, peppermint sticks,
   dried apricots, cookies, pretzels and JET-PUFFED®
   Marshmallows
4 squares BAKER'S® Premium White Baking Chocolate, melted
   (optional)

MICROWAVE chocolate in small microwavable bowl on HIGH
2 minutes or until chocolate is almost melted. Stir until chocolate is
completely melted.

DIP dippers into chocolate; let excess chocolate drip off. Let stand at
room temperature or refrigerate on wax paper-lined cookie sheet
30 minutes or until chocolate is firm. Drizzle with melted white
chocolate, if desired.   *Makes about 2 dozen dippers*

Great Substitute: Prepare as directed, substituting 1 package (6 squares)
BAKER'S® Bittersweet Baking Chocolate *or* 1 package (6 squares)
BAKER'S® Premium White Baking Chocolate for Sweet or Semi-Sweet
Chocolate.

Prep Time: 30 minutes plus cooling

Chocolate Dipped Delights

White Chocolate Bread Pudding

1 package (6 ounces) BAKER'S® Premium White Baking Chocolate

2 cups half-and-half *or* milk

1/2 cup sugar

1/4 cup (1/2 stick) butter *or* margarine

3 eggs, lightly beaten

2 teaspoons vanilla

5 cups white bread cubes (1/2-inch)

Boiling water

Chocolate Sauce (recipe follows)

HEAT oven to 325°F.

MICROWAVE chocolate, half-and-half, sugar and butter in large microwavable bowl on HIGH 4 minutes, stirring halfway through heating time. Stir until chocolate is completely melted. Beat in eggs and vanilla. Pour over bread cubes in 2-quart baking dish. Place dish in larger baking pan, then place in oven. Carefully pour boiling water into pan to come 1 inch up side of baking dish.

BAKE 40 to 45 minutes or until knife inserted near center comes out almost clean. Serve warm with Chocolate Sauce.   *Makes 8 servings*

Chocolate Sauce: Microwave 1 package (8 squares) BAKER'S® Semi-Sweet Baking Chocolate and 1 cup whipping (heavy) cream in large microwavable bowl on HIGH 4 minutes until cream is simmering, stirring halfway through heating time. Stir with wire whisk until chocolate is melted and mixture is smooth. Makes 1 1/2 cups.

Prep Time: 15 minutes
Bake Time: 45 minutes

Chocolate Minute® Tapioca Pudding

3 squares BAKER'S® Semi-Sweet Baking Chocolate, chopped

$^1/_3$ cup sugar

3 tablespoons MINUTE® Tapioca

3 cups milk

1 egg, well beaten

1 teaspoon vanilla

MIX chocolate, sugar, tapioca, milk and egg in medium saucepan. Let stand 5 minutes.

COOK on medium heat, stirring constantly, until mixture comes to full boil. (Pudding thickens as it cools.) Remove from heat. Stir in vanilla.

COOL 20 minutes; stir. Serve warm or chilled.

Makes 6 ($^1/_2$-cup) servings

Special Extras: Garnish with thawed COOL WHIP® Whipped Topping and grated BAKER'S® Semi-Sweet Baking Chocolate.

Prep Time: 5 minutes
Cook Time: 10 minutes

Chocolate Plunge

$^2/_3$ cup light corn syrup

$^1/_2$ cup whipping (heavy) cream

1 package (8 squares) BAKER'S® Semi-Sweet Baking Chocolate
   or 2 packages (4 ounces each) BAKER'S® GERMAN'S®
   Sweet Chocolate

Assorted fresh fruit (strawberries, sliced kiwi fruit, pineapple,
   apple or banana), cookies, pound cake cubes or pretzels

MICROWAVE corn syrup and cream in large microwavable bowl on
HIGH 1$^1/_2$ minutes or until mixture comes to boil. Add chocolate; stir
until completely melted.

SERVE warm as dip with assorted fresh fruit, cookies, cake cubes or
pretzels.   *Makes 1$^1/_2$ cups*

Chocolate Peanut Butter Plunge: Stir in $^1/_2$ cup peanut butter with
chocolate.

Chocolate Raspberry Plunge: Stir in $^1/_4$ cup seedless raspberry jam with
chocolate.

Mocha Plunge: Stir in 1 tablespoon MAXWELL HOUSE® Instant
Coffee with chocolate.

Prep Time: 5 minutes

Chocolate Plunge

Gift-Giving Indulgence

Give these delicious gifts from the kitchen—truffles, fudge, biscotti and more—to show those you love how much you care.

Chocolate-Dipped
Coconut Macaroons

 1 package (14 ounces) BAKER'S® ANGEL FLAKE® Coconut
    (5 1/3 cups)
 2/3 cup sugar
 6 tablespoons flour
 1/4 teaspoon salt
 4 egg whites
 1 teaspoon almond extract
 1 package (8 squares) BAKER'S® Semi-Sweet Baking Chocolate,
    melted

HEAT oven to 325°F.

MIX coconut, sugar, flour and salt in large bowl. Stir in egg whites and almond extract until well blended. Drop by teaspoonfuls onto greased and floured cookie sheets.

BAKE 20 minutes or until edges of cookies are golden brown. Immediately remove from cookie sheets to wire racks and cool completely. Dip cookies halfway into melted chocolate. Let stand at room temperature or refrigerate on wax paper-lined tray 30 minutes or until chocolate is firm.   *Makes about 3 dozen cookies*

Storage Know-How: Store in tightly covered container up to 1 week.

Prep Time: 15 minutes
Bake Time: 20 minutes

Holiday Marble Bark

6 squares BAKER'S® Semi-Sweet Baking Chocolate *or* 1 package
(6 squares) BAKER'S® Bittersweet Baking Chocolate

1 package (6 squares) BAKER'S® Premium White Baking
Chocolate

1 cup crushed peppermint candies (about 50 peppermint starlight
candies)

MICROWAVE semi-sweet and white chocolates in separate medium
microwavable bowls on HIGH 2 minutes or until chocolates are almost
melted, stirring halfway through heating time. Stir until chocolates are
completely melted.

STIR 1/2 cup of the peppermint candies into each bowl. Alternately spoon
melted chocolates onto wax paper-lined cookie sheet. Swirl chocolates
together with knife to marbleize.

REFRIGERATE 1 hour or until firm. Break into pieces.

Makes about 1 pound

How to crush peppermint candies: Place candies in zipper-style plastic
bag. Crush with rolling pin or mallet. Or, process in food processor using
pulsing action.

Make-Ahead: Can be prepared up to 3 weeks ahead for gift-giving. Store
in an airtight container between layers of wax paper in the refrigerator.

Chocolate Peanut Butter Marble Bark: Prepare as directed, omitting
peppermint candies. Stir 1/4 cup creamy peanut butter into melted white
chocolate.

Chocolate Nut Marble Bark: Prepare as directed, substituting 1 cup toasted chopped nuts *or* toasted BAKER'S® ANGEL FLAKE® Coconut for peppermint candies.

Festive Fruit Bark: Prepare as directed, omitting Semi-Sweet Chocolate and peppermint. Use 2 packages (6 squares each) BAKER'S® Premium White Chocolate. Stir in $1/2$ cup dried cranberries and $1/2$ cup toasted chopped almonds *or* pistachios.

Prep Time: 20 minutes
Refrigerate Time: 1 hour

Regal Chocolate Sauce

   2 squares BAKER'S® Unsweetened Baking Chocolate
$1/3$ cup water
$1/2$ cup sugar
   3 tablespoons butter *or* margarine
$1/4$ teaspoon vanilla

MICROWAVE chocolate and water in large microwavable bowl on HIGH $1^{1}/2$ minutes. Stir until chocolate is completely melted.

STIR sugar into chocolate mixture. Microwave 3 minutes until sugar is completely dissolved, stirring halfway through heating time. Stir in butter and vanilla.   *Makes about 1 cup sauce*

Regal Mocha Sauce: Stir in 1 tablespoon MAXWELL HOUSE® Instant Coffee with sugar.

Prep Time: 5 minutes

Dark Chocolate Fudge

$^1/_2$ cup light *or* dark corn syrup

$^1/_3$ cup evaporated milk *or* whipping (heavy) cream

2 packages (8 squares each) BAKER'S® Semi-Sweet Baking
Chocolate

$^3/_4$ cup powdered sugar, sifted

2 teaspoons vanilla

1 cup coarsely chopped nuts (optional)

LINE 8-inch square baking pan with foil; grease foil.

HEAT corn syrup, evaporated milk and chocolate in 2-quart saucepan on medium-low heat until chocolate is melted, stirring constantly. Remove from heat.

STIR in sugar, vanilla and nuts. Beat with wooden spoon until thick and glossy. Immediately spread in prepared pan.

REFRIGERATE 2 hours or until firm. Let stand at room temperature 15 minutes before cutting into 1-inch squares. *Makes 64 pieces*

Make-Ahead: Can be prepared up to 3 weeks ahead for gift-giving. Store in an airtight container between layers of wax paper in the refrigerator.

Prep Time: 10 minutes
Refrigerate Time: 2 hours

Dark Chocolate Fudge, Chocolate Truffles (page 115) and Holiday Marble Bark (page 106)

White Chocolate Cranberry Biscotti

2 cups flour

1 1/2 teaspoons CALUMET® Baking Powder

1/4 teaspoon salt

1/2 cup (1 stick) butter *or* margarine, softened

1/2 cup sugar

2 eggs

1 teaspoon vanilla

1 package (12 ounces) BAKER'S® White Chocolate Chunks, divided

1/2 cup dried cranberries

1/2 cup chopped pecans (optional)

HEAT oven to 325°F. Lightly grease and flour large cookie sheet. Mix flour, baking powder and salt in medium bowl; set aside.

BEAT butter and sugar in large bowl with electric mixer on medium speed until light and fluffy. Add eggs and vanilla; beat well. Gradually beat in flour mixture. Stir in 1 1/2 cups of the chocolate chunks, cranberries and pecans.

DIVIDE dough into 2 equal portions. On floured board, shape dough into 2 logs, each 14 inches long, 1 1/2 inches wide and 1 inch thick. Place 2 inches apart on prepared cookie sheet.

BAKE 25 to 28 minutes or until lightly browned. Cool on cookie sheet 15 minutes. On cutting board, cut each log with serrated knife into diagonal slices about 3/4 inch thick. Place slices, cut sides down, on cookie sheet 1/2 inch apart. Bake 10 minutes or until slightly dry. Remove to wire racks and cool completely.

MELT remaining chocolate chunks as directed on package. Drizzle over biscotti. Let stand until chocolate is firm. *Makes about 3 dozen cookies*

Storage Know-How: Store in tightly covered container up to 2 weeks.

Prep Time: 30 minutes
Bake Time: 38 minutes

Pastel Marble Bark

2 packages (6 squares each) BAKER'S® Premium White Baking
   Chocolate
Assorted food colorings (see below)

MICROWAVE each package of chocolate in separate medium microwavable bowls on HIGH 2 minutes or until chocolates are almost melted, stirring halfway through heating time. Stir until chocolates are completely melted.

STIR different food coloring into each bowl of melted chocolate until well blended (or, tint just 1 bowl of chocolate, keeping second bowl of chocolate white). Alternately spoon tinted chocolates onto wax paper-lined cookie sheet or tray. Tap cookie sheet on tabletop to evenly disperse chocolate. Swirl chocolates with knife to marbleize.

REFRIGERATE 1 hour or until firm. Break into pieces.

Makes about 1 pound

Tip: To tint 1 package (6 squares) BAKER'S® Premium White Baking Chocolate, use the following amounts of food coloring: pink: 3 drops red, pastel green: 3 drops green, pastel yellow: 3 drops yellow, pastel blue: 5 drops blue.

Prep Time: 20 minutes

Chocolate Chunk Banana Bread Mix

2 cups flour

1 cup sugar

1 cup BAKER'S® Semi-Sweet Chocolate Chunks

1/2 cup chopped nuts

2 teaspoons CALUMET® Baking Powder

1/4 teaspoon salt

LAYER all dry ingredients in 5-cup glass container or jar. Tap jar gently on counter to settle each layer before adding next one. Cover.

ATTACH baking directions (see below).

BAKING DIRECTIONS

HEAT oven to 350°F. Grease 9×5-inch loaf pan. Stir **1 cup mashed ripe bananas, 2 eggs, 1/3 cup oil** and **1/4 cup milk** in large bowl until well blended. Empty contents of jar into bowl. Stir until well mixed. Pour into prepared pan.

BAKE 55 minutes or until toothpick inserted in center comes out clean. Cool completely in pan on wire rack. *Makes 1 loaf*

Prep Time: 5 minutes

Chocolate Chunk Banana Bread Mix and Sure-Jell® Cranberry Strawberry Jam
(page 114)

Sure-Jell® Cranberry Strawberry Jam

 1 bag (12 ounces) fresh cranberries
 1 package (16 ounces) frozen sliced strawberries in sugar, thawed
 1 box SURE-JELL® Fruit Pectin
 ½ teaspoon butter *or* margarine (optional)
 3¾ cups sugar, measured into separate bowl (see tip below)

WASH jars and screw bands in hot, soapy water; rinse with warm water. Pour boiling water over flat lids in saucepan off the heat. Let stand in hot water until ready to use. Drain well before filling.

CHOP cranberries in food processor using pulsing action; place in 6- or 8-quart saucepot. Add strawberries to saucepot.

STIR pectin into prepared fruit in saucepot. Add butter to reduce foaming, if desired. Bring mixture to full rolling boil (a boil that doesn't stop bubbling when stirred) on high heat, stirring constantly.

STIR in all sugar. Return to full rolling boil and boil exactly 1 minute, stirring constantly. Remove from heat. Skim off any foam with metal spoon.

LADLE quickly into prepared jars, filling to within ⅛ inch of tops. Wipe jar rims and threads. Cover with two-piece lids. Screw bands tightly. Invert jars 5 minutes, then turn upright. Or, follow water bath method recommended by USDA. After jars are cool, check seals.   *Makes about 5 (1-cup) jars*

Important Tip: To get exact *level* cup measures of sugar, spoon sugar into dry measuring cup, then level by scraping excess sugar from top of cup with a straight-edged knife.

Prep Time: 45 minutes

Chocolate Truffles

1 package (8 squares) BAKER'S® Semi-Sweet Baking Chocolate

4 ounces (¹/₂ of 8-ounce package) PHILADELPHIA® Cream
    Cheese, softened

1 tub (8 ounces) COOL WHIP® Whipped Topping, thawed
    Powdered sugar, finely chopped nuts, toasted BAKER'S®
    ANGEL FLAKE® Coconut, grated BAKER'S® Semi-Sweet
    Baking Chocolate, cookie crumbs *or* multi-colored sprinkles

MICROWAVE chocolate in large microwavable bowl on HIGH
2 minutes or until chocolate is almost melted. Stir until chocolate is
completely melted.

STIR cream cheese into chocolate mixture with wire whisk until well
blended and smooth. Cool to room temperature. Gently stir in whipped
topping.

REFRIGERATE 1 hour. Shape into 1-inch balls. Roll in powdered
sugar, nuts, coconut, grated chocolate, cookie crumbs or sprinkles. Store in
refrigerator.   *Makes about 2¹/₂ to 3 dozen truffles*

Variation: Prepare as directed except for refrigerating. Freeze 1 hour.
Scoop into 1-inch balls. If necessary, freeze 30 minutes longer or until
firm enough to roll in coating. Store in refrigerator.

Gift-Giving Tip: Place truffles in paper candy cups and pack in a
decorative gift box.

Prep Time: 15 minutes
Refrigerate Time: 1 hour

Chocolate Almond Biscotti

1 package (12 ounces) BAKER'S® Semi-Sweet Chocolate Chunks, divided

2 cups flour

1 1/2 teaspoons CALUMET® Baking Powder

1/4 teaspoon salt

1/4 cup (1/2 stick) butter *or* margarine, softened

1/2 cup granulated sugar

1/2 cup firmly packed brown sugar

3 eggs

1 teaspoon vanilla

1 cup slivered almonds, toasted

HEAT oven to 325°F. Lightly grease and flour large cookie sheet. Reserve 1/2 cup chocolate chunks. Microwave remaining chocolate chunks in small microwavable bowl on HIGH 2 minutes. Stir until chocolate is completely melted; cool slightly. Mix flour, baking powder and salt in medium bowl; set aside.

BEAT butter and sugars in large bowl with electric mixer on medium speed until well blended. Add eggs, 1 at a time, beating well after each addition. Beat in melted chocolate and vanilla. Gradually beat in flour mixture. Stir in almonds.

DIVIDE dough into 2 equal portions. On floured board, shape dough into 2 logs, each 10 inches long, 2 inches wide and 1 inch thick. Place 2 inches apart on prepared cookie sheet.

BAKE 40 to 50 minutes or until toothpick inserted in center of each log comes out clean. Cool on cookie sheet 15 minutes. On cutting board, cut each log with serrated knife into diagonal slices about 3/4 inch thick. Place slices, cut sides down, on cookie sheet. Bake 20 minutes, turning biscotti over halfway through baking time. Remove to wire racks and cool completely.

MELT reserved chocolate chunks as directed on package. Drizzle over biscotti. Let stand until chocolate is firm.   *Makes about 3 dozen cookies*

Storage Know-How: Store in tightly covered container up to 2 weeks.

Prep Time: 30 minutes
Bake Time: 70 minutes

Chocolate Almond Biscotti and White Chocolate Cranberry Biscotti (page 110)

Cappuccino Chocolate Chunk Muffin Mix

2 cups flour

1 cup BAKER'S® Semi-Sweet Chocolate Chunks

$^1/_2$ cup sugar

$^1/_2$ cup GENERAL FOODS INTERNATIONAL COFFEES®,
   any flavor

$2^1/_2$ teaspoons CALUMET® Baking Powder

$^1/_2$ teaspoon cinnamon

$^1/_2$ teaspoon salt

PLACE all ingredients in 1-gallon zipper-style plastic bag. Close tightly. Place in decorative gift bag. Attach baking directions (see below).

BAKING DIRECTIONS

HEAT oven to 375°F. Grease or line muffin pan with papers. Beat **1 egg** in large bowl; stir in **1 cup milk** and **$^1/_2$ cup (1 stick) butter _or_ margarine, melted.** Empty contents of bag into bowl. Stir just until moistened. Spoon batter into prepared muffin pan, filling each cup $^2/_3$ full.

BAKE 15 to 20 minutes or until toothpick inserted in center of muffin comes out clean. Cool 5 minutes; remove from pan. Cool completely on wire rack.   _Makes 1 dozen muffins_

Prep Time: 10 minutes

Bittersweet Chocolate Truffle Squares

$^3/_4$ cup whipping (heavy) cream

$^1/_4$ cup ($^1/_2$ stick) butter *or* margarine, cut into chunks

3 tablespoons sugar

2 packages (6 squares each) BAKER'S® Bittersweet Baking Chocolate, broken into chunks

$^1/_2$ teaspoon vanilla

1 cup finely chopped toasted almonds

LINE 8-inch square baking pan with foil.

MICROWAVE cream, butter and sugar in large microwavable bowl on HIGH 3 minutes until mixture comes to full boil, stirring halfway through heating time. Add chocolate and vanilla; stir until chocolate is completely melted.

REFRIGERATE about 2 hours or until firm enough to handle. Sprinkle almonds in bottom of prepared pan. Spread chocolate mixture evenly over almonds. Refrigerate 2 hours or until firm. Cut into squares.

Makes 4 dozen squares

Make-Ahead: Can be prepared up to 3 weeks ahead for gift-giving. Store in an airtight container between layers of wax paper in the refrigerator.

Bittersweet Chocolate Truffle Balls: Prepare as directed, omitting almonds, shaping mixture into 1-inch balls. Roll in cocoa, BAKER'S® ANGEL FLAKE® Coconut, cookie crumbs or nuts. Store in refrigerator. Makes about 2 dozen truffle balls.

Prep Time: 15 minutes
Refrigerate Time: 4 hours

METRIC CONVERSION CHART

VOLUME MEASUREMENTS (dry)

$\frac{1}{8}$ teaspoon = 0.5 mL
$\frac{1}{4}$ teaspoon = 1 mL
$\frac{1}{2}$ teaspoon = 2 mL
$\frac{3}{4}$ teaspoon = 4 mL
1 teaspoon = 5 mL
1 tablespoon = 15 mL
2 tablespoons = 30 mL
$\frac{1}{4}$ cup = 60 mL
$\frac{1}{3}$ cup = 75 mL
$\frac{1}{2}$ cup = 125 mL
$\frac{2}{3}$ cup = 150 mL
$\frac{3}{4}$ cup = 175 mL
1 cup = 250 mL
2 cups = 1 pint = 500 mL
3 cups = 750 mL
4 cups = 1 quart = 1 L

VOLUME MEASUREMENTS (fluid)

1 fluid ounce (2 tablespoons) = 30 mL
4 fluid ounces ($\frac{1}{2}$ cup) = 125 mL
8 fluid ounces (1 cup) = 250 mL
12 fluid ounces (1$\frac{1}{2}$ cups) = 375 mL
16 fluid ounces (2 cups) = 500 mL

WEIGHTS (mass)

$\frac{1}{2}$ ounce = 15 g
1 ounce = 30 g
3 ounces = 90 g
4 ounces = 120 g
8 ounces = 225 g
10 ounces = 285 g
12 ounces = 360 g
16 ounces = 1 pound = 450 g

DIMENSIONS

$\frac{1}{16}$ inch = 2 mm
$\frac{1}{8}$ inch = 3 mm
$\frac{1}{4}$ inch = 6 mm
$\frac{1}{2}$ inch = 1.5 cm
$\frac{3}{4}$ inch = 2 cm
1 inch = 2.5 cm

OVEN TEMPERATURES

250°F = 120°C
275°F = 140°C
300°F = 150°C
325°F = 160°C
350°F = 180°C
375°F = 190°C
400°F = 200°C
425°F = 220°C
450°F = 230°C

BAKING PAN SIZES

Utensil	Size in Inches/Quarts	Metric Volume	Size in Centimeters
Baking or Cake Pan (square or rectangular)	8×8×2	2 L	20×20×5
	9×9×2	2.5 L	23×23×5
	12×8×2	3 L	30×20×5
	13×9×2	3.5 L	33×23×5
Loaf Pan	8×4×3	1.5 L	20×10×7
	9×5×3	2 L	23×13×7
Round Layer Cake Pan	8×1½	1.2 L	20×4
	9×1½	1.5 L	23×4
Pie Plate	8×1¼	750 mL	20×3
	9×1¼	1 L	23×3
Baking Dish or Casserole	1 quart	1 L	—
	1½ quart	1.5 L	—
	2 quart	2 L	—